English History

Strange but True

English history

Strange but True

Richard Smyth

The
History
Press

First published 2014

The History Press
The Mill, Brimscombe Port
Stroud, Gloucestershire, GL5 2QG
www.thehistorypress.co.uk

British Library Cataloguing in Publication Data.
A catalogue record for this book is available from the British Library.

ISBN 978 0 7524 9970 3

Typesetting and origination by The History Press and Printed in Malta by Melita Press
Production managed by Jellyfish

Contents

Introduction

This is a book about England. We shan't venture north of Hadrian's Wall – for didn't Scotland's own king, Alexander II, say that 'ungovernable, wild men dwell there, who thirst after human blood, and whom I myself cannot tame'? He did indeed, in 1237, to a papal legate in England on pontifical business. Nor shall we stray too far west, into Wales – the kingdom known to the Romans as 'Britannia Secunda', or 'secondary Britain'.

No, we shall remain in England – that land known to seventeenth-century Italians as 'the paradise of women, the purgatory of servants, and the hell of horses' – the country of St George, Richard the Lionheart and Queen Victoria (except that Victoria was mostly German, Richard entirely French, and St George Palestinian, if indeed he existed at all).

It's also a book about the English; those fine, upright people in whom Pope Gregory the Great famously saw 'not Angles, but Angels' – an observation made, by the by, while he was eyeing up slave boys in one of Rome's marketplaces.

Most of all, this is a book of stories. Some are gruesome. Some are funny. Most are unbelievable. All are true. This is what history gets up to when it thinks no one's looking.

Prehistory

or, Really Really Really REALLY Olde England

Complete this sentence: Nelson's column is to the hippopotamus as Stonehenge is to ___. Give up? Answer at the end of the chapter …

Contrary to what your schoolbooks and National Trust tea towels might have told you, English history didn't begin with William the Conqueror, Duke of Normandy. English history began, not with a Norman, but with a Roger.

Roger was a pretty average individual: he stood around 5ft 11in, lived in south-east England and died – alas – at the age of around 40. Strictly speaking, Roger wasn't human, but nobody's perfect.

Roger lived near the pleasant West Sussex village of Boxgrove (good schools, pretty church, Zumba classes in the village hall every Thursday). We don't know much more about him than that. But then, how much will people know about you in half a million years' time? Roger lived near Boxgrove around 500,000 years ago. That's practically before humans were invented.

Roger was a specimen of the pre-human species *Homo heidelbergiensis*, and is known as 'Boxgrove Man', which doesn't quite tell the whole story; a better name would be 'Boxgrove Shin', as that's all that was left of Roger when we found him. Everything else we know about him has been figured out through expert analysis, beginning with 'the shin bone's connected to the knee bone' and proceeding from there. We don't know very much about Roger's day-to-day habits, although we do know that he was found in the vicinity of a butchered rhino pelvis. Make of that what you will.

As for the 'Roger', that can be attributed to the peculiar whims of archaeologists. England's oldest man was named after his discoverer, Danish bone-boffin Roger Pedersen, who unearthed the shin-bone in November 1993.

Contemplating our ancient history can be mind-bending. For most of recorded history, we have simply had no idea how incredibly venerable we are – as a species, as a planet, and as trace elements in a 13.7-billion-year-old universe.

The seventeenth-century Irish archbishop James Ussher famously used Biblical scripture as evidence that the world was created in 4004 BC, and has been vigorously derided for it ever since.

But he was far from alone in massively underestimating the amount of time we humans have so far spent here on earth. The challenge of contemplating prehistory was certainly too much for the antiquarian John Bayford, who, upon finding elephant bones and an ancient spear point near Gray's Inn Road in London in 1715, assumed that the spear point had been used to kill one of Emperor Claudius' elephants on the Romans' entry into Britain in AD 43. He was around 398,000 years out.

It's true: elephants roamed free in prehistoric England. Long before even old Roger de Boxgrove arrived on the scene, around 900,000 years ago, the swamps of south-east England abounded with hippos and elephants. 700,000 years ago, England's climate was more Mediterranean than Nordic; 400,000 years ago, early humans dwelt on the banks of the mile-wide Thames among rhinoceros, lions,

macaque monkeys, dolphins, straight-tusked elephant, bison, giant oxen, and wolves. Meanwhile at West Stow, in Suffolk, prehistoric whiz-kids came up with a new-fangled invention called 'fire'.

It all makes it seem as though the events we think of as 'history' happened only yesterday. London looks and feels like an old city, but it's been there for barely an eye blink, compared to the prehistoric bones that have been found beneath it: woolly mammoths down the Strand, reindeer at South Kensington station, rhinoceros at Battersea power station, and – as though to cock a snook at our ideas of what constitutes 'history' – hippos in Trafalgar Square, in the shadow of that 'historical' figure Lord Nelson.

Taking the long view, a hippopotamus is a far more representative icon of England's history than the decidedly modern Nelson. Now there's an idea for that fourth plinth.

The first breakthrough in unearthing our prehistory came not in London, but in Yorkshire (where history is history, and don't you bloody forget it). Kirkland Cave, high in the Dales, was examined in 1822 by the Oxford academic William Buckland – who found it strewn with exotic animal bones. Buckland surmised that the cave had been home to prehistoric hyenas, and was therefore littered with their leftovers (exploding an alternative thesis that attributed the presence of the bones to the Great Flood of Genesis).

Buckland was so enraptured by his hyena hypothesis that he adopted one as a household pet. He called it 'Billy'. It had a habit of upsetting house guests by noisily crunching guinea pigs under the settee.

We can't leave the splendid and flowingly berobed William Buckland without telling a couple more stories about him.

One tale recounts that, in order to investigate the provenance of the fossilised reptile footprints found in Dumfriesshire in the 1820s, Buckland and his colleagues induced a tortoise to walk through wet pie crust. 'It was really a glorious sight,' wrote the publisher John Murray, 'to behold all the philosophers, flour-besmeared, working away with tucked-up sleeves.'

Another concerns Buckland's all-encompassing appetite – and his stated ambition of eating every species of creature on earth. A conservative modern estimate would put that at around 3 million species, so to achieve his peculiar aim, Buckland would have had to munch his way through at least 100 species a day, every day of his life – but he certainly had a good stab at it, sampling such treats as bluebottles, toasted mice, panthers and puppies, among many other creatures (sadly, his recipe book has been lost to posterity).

The apogee of Buckland's gastronomical adventuring, though, came during a high-toned dinner at Nuneham House in Oxfordshire. The meal having been concluded, his host, evidently a collector of curiosities, was proudly showing off the jewel of his collection: the embalmed and somewhat shrunken heart of Louis XIV of France, the 'Sun King', the grandest monarch of his (and perhaps any) age. Buckland was impressed. He was also, it seems, still hungry. 'I have eaten many strange things,' he remarked, 'but have never eaten the heart of a king before.' Before anyone could stop him, Buckland had gulped down the nut-sized royal offal in one.

His host was left to reflect that perhaps this is what comes of being stingy with the portions at dinner.

Now let's get bang up-to-date by taking a look at a well-known example of cutting-edge contemporary architecture: Stonehenge. (What? Even by the most extreme estimates, the construction of Stonehenge is far nearer to us than to Roger de Boxgrove – when he passed on, Stonehenge was still at least 400,000 years in the future, making it as outlandish to him as architecture of the year 402,014 would seem to us.)

The name of Stonehenge is, of course, famous around the world. But the reason why we call the monument 'Stonehenge' is less well known, and a bit grim. The name means 'hanging stones'. It was thought in the Middle Ages that the huge crossed 'trilithons' were used not as a calendar or a solar clock or even a set of impromptu goalposts – but as a gallows.

But let's get down to brass tacks. 5,000 years of history is all very well – but how much would you pay for a few blocks of Cenozoic silcrete, a nice bit of rhyolitic tuff and an unworked sarsen stone? In 1915, Cecil Chubb paid £6,600 – and became the last owner of Stonehenge. 'I thought a Salisbury man ought to buy it and that is how it was done,' he said. In 1918, though, he generously gave it back to the nation.

Now, that question we began with: Nelson's column is to the hippopotamus as Stonehenge is to what? The answer, discovered only recently, shook England to its very foundations. It is: the frog.

In 2013, frog bones from thousands of years before Stonehenge was built were discovered buried near the ancient stones, just as those ancient hippo remains were excavated in Trafalgar Square. But these were not any old frog bones. They had been cooked (and possibly breadcrumbed)! This led archaeologists to a shocking conclusion: the English had been eating frogs' legs. In fact, it seems that the English invented it between 7,000 and 9,000 years ago, long before it occurred to anyone else. Zut alors!

Roman England

or, All Woads Lead to Rome

For a long time, the Romans were pretty sure that there was no such thing as England. There were rumours among mariners and traders of a rainy archipelago, north-west of Gaul, rich in lead and tin – but the historian Herodotus, writing of these so-called 'Tin Islands', sniffed: 'I do not believe they exist.'

Once the Romans found their way to the top end of Gaul and got a look at the English coast for themselves, they let their imaginations get the better of them. They imagined that they had discovered 'an island of which the shores abounded with pearls, and the soil with ores of the more precious metals'.

But no. It was mostly lead and tin. Later exports included skins, dogs, and slaves – which the Britons exchanged for pottery and salt.

There followed a series of unimpressive attempts to conquer Britain by a succession of emperors whose hearts weren't really in it. Most laughable of all was the 'effort' made by Caligula in around AD 40. This ridiculous Roman assembled his legions on the beach at Boulogne in France, had himself rowed briefly out into the Channel and then hastily back again, and declared that Rome had 'conquered the sea'.

He then told his men to gather seashells from the Boulogne beach, as proof of their conquest. Across the sea, the Britons kept calm and carried on.

It wasn't until AD 43 that the Romans finally got round to launching an invasion worthy of the name. It was a fierce and purposeful assault, and the naked, woad-smeared Britons – whose guerrilla tactics had proved sufficient to see off Julius Caesar around 100 years before – stood little chance.

But this was only partly a Roman conquest. For one thing, the troops who really did the damage were not Roman legionaries but German auxiliaries; the Germans, unlike the disciplined Romans, were adept at taking on the Britons at their own game, and accustomed to scrapping in northern European conditions.

What's more, the invasion, though led by Aulus Plautius, had been instigated not by a Roman or even by a German but by – gasp! – a Brit – one Beric, who, as a result of internal squabbling among the tribes of the Tin Islands, had been exiled from his native land.

A word about woad. Woad was, of course, the blue dye with which the Britons liked to slather themselves before going into battle. But woad didn't die out with the ancient British culture; fermented and mixed with urine, it provided English textile makers with blue dye for centuries afterward.

By the sixteenth century, we actually had too much woad. The mass cultivation of woad plants (*Isatis tinctoria*) was eating into grain production, and had to be restricted by the government. Elizabeth I later lifted these restrictions (but still wouldn't allow any woad-processing plants near her palaces, because she found the stench unbearable). The last woad mill in England closed in 1932.

The ancient Britons also used woad to tattoo themselves. 'The Briton was vain of this hideous ornament,' one historian has sniffily noted, 'and to exhibit it before the eyes of his enemies, he was always careful to throw off his clothes on the day of battle.'

The ancient Britons were, of course, followers of the Druidic religion, about which we know very little. It was mostly to do with mistletoe and human sacrifice.

The Druids did influence modern society in one very specific (and rather morbid) way – or anyway, a Druid did. He did so in 1884. For the avoidance of doubt, that's AD 1884. William Price was a devout Druid. He refused to wear socks and frowned upon marriage and meat-eating. All well and good. Then, in 1884, Price's son died, and Price took the body to a Welsh hilltop and tried to set it on fire.

But such Druidical practices had fallen out of favour in the 1,800 years or so since the religion's heyday. Price found himself in court. 'It is not right,' he protested, 'that a carcass should be allowed to rot and decompose. It results in a wastage of good land, pollution of the earth, water and air, and is a constant danger to all living creatures.'

He was acquitted. Cremation, the judge ruled, was not an offence – and so Price the Druid, in pursuing his ancient way of life, transformed our way of death.

It wouldn't be quite right to say that people were queuing up to be cremated after that, but in 1885, the body of one

Mrs Pickersgill was consigned to the flames at a Woking crematorium. It was the first official cremation in the UK since pre-Roman times.

Having invaded and made themselves at home, the Romans didn't get things all their own way. Enter Boudicca, widow of the Iceni king (and Roman ally) Prasutagus. After Prasutagus' death in around AD 60, the Romans reneged on their agreements with the Iceni and plundered the king's estates. When Boudicca protested, she was flogged and her daughters raped.

70,000 Romans – and Roman sympathisers, who were considered just as guilty – were killed in the ensuing revolt. London and St Albans (the principal city of early Roman Britain) were ravaged. It was a horrendously bloody business. 'The Britons,' wrote the Roman Tacitus, 'took no prisoners … [and] wasted no time in getting down to the bloody business of hanging, burning, and crucifying.'

It all came to an end when Suetonius' 10,000 Romans quashed the revolting Brits in a battle somewhere in the Midlands. Suetonius supposedly outdid the rebels in butchery: the British death toll was estimated at 80,000.

Boudicca escaped the slaughter, but died soon afterwards (it's probable she was poisoned). 'Boudicca', by the way, is best rendered into modern English as 'Victoria'. She was our first Queen Victoria – and she too, it's fair to say, was not amused.

Just as they'd harassed the invading Romans to distraction, the Celtic Britons did their best to resist the advances of the fierce and piratical Saxons, Angles and Jutes, who late in the fourth century started bothering the English coastline in a

determined manner that suggested they might intend to stay around for a while. The British soldiers fought back with chariot, spear – and shouting.

Shouting, on at least one occasion, was a more effective weapon than you might imagine. In the fifth century, a force of Britons (led by a Gallic bishop, Germanus) travelled to the south coast to confront an army of marauding Saxons. The Brits waited in ambush for the trespassers – and then, as they approached, 'raised a general shout of "'Hallelujah!''' The cry, it is said, echoed around the surrounding hills, and scared the bejeezus out of the Saxons. They fled in reckless disarray – and many perished in a nearby river.

This strange incident became known as 'the Hallelujah Victory'. It was also, given the years of Anglo-Saxon dominance that followed, something of a final hurrah for the Celtic Brits.

Anglo-Saxon England

or, Wessex Girls Do It in the Dark Ages

The post-Roman, pre-Norman period is English history's equivalent to that awkward bit of the twentieth century that came after rock 'n' roll but before the Beatles. It's generally given the dismissive sobriquet 'the Dark Ages', which leads many people to think that nothing at all of interest happened then. This is simply a case of bad branding.

But actually, it's pretty typical of the so-called Dark Ages to end up with a duff nickname. English rulers of the period made rather a habit of it. At around the time that the Vikings were rallying round Erik 'Bloodaxe' and Harald 'Greycloak', for example, Essex was being ruled by a man called Sigebert the Little.

This isn't to say, however, that the Vikings always got it right. One of their greatest leaders in the ninth century was known as Ivar the Boneless, as though he were some sort of oven-ready Norse fillet rather than the man who invaded England at the head of the Great Heathen Army in AD 865. Ivar's grandson came off even worse: could you be introduced to a man named Sihtric the Squint-Eyed and not start giggling, even if he was the Viking King of York? Another Viking invader, Thorgils Skarthi, 'the Harelipped', not only overcame the embarrassment of having a needlessly personal nickname, but even ended up having a whole town named after him: the seaside resort of Scarborough.

But of course, there were worse things that could befall a Dark Ages monarch than being lumbered with a silly name …

King Oswald ruled the vast Christian kingdom of Northumbria in the seventh century. The Northumbrians had an ongoing

beef with the Mercians of middle England (by which we mean
that they lived in the middle of England, i.e. in the Midlands –
not that they were comfortably well-off and read the *Daily Mail*).

At Maserfield (probably somewhere in Shropshire,
and probably in AD 641 or 642 – welcome to Dark Ages
history!), the Mercians, under their formidable pagan chieftain
Penda, gave the Northumbrians a damn good thrashing. Oswald
was captured, chopped into pieces, and hung from a tree.

Oswald's brother Oswy came down to Maserfield a year
later to collect what was left of the ex-king's body. For some
reason, he decided that Oswald's head was the only bit worth
keeping, so he took that with him back to Lindisfarne and left
the rest where it was. (Shortly afterwards, Penda got hacked
to death by Northumbrians on a muddy riverbank in Leeds,
so justice was done, in a Dark Ages sort of way.)

Looking on the bright side for Oswald, at least he was dead and
in pieces when the Mercians hung him from a tree. Edmund
of East Anglia wasn't so lucky.

When the Vikings got hold of Edmund in AD 869, they
ordered him to renounce his Christian faith – or suffer the
consequences. When he refused, the Viking leader Ivar showed
himself to be not only Boneless but also Ruthless, Merciless
and Heartless: he had Edmund tied to a tree, and told his
archers to use him for target practice. Then, for good measure,
they chopped his head off and chucked it into the forest.[1]

Eventually, the Dark Ages threw up a king we could be proud
of – and who had a first-class nickname, to boot. Alfred the
Great, King of Wessex, was, it's well known, pretty good at

seeing off Johnny Viking. He was also a distant last in the Great Wessex Bake-Off of AD 871. What's less well known is that, as well as being the scourge of the Norsemen, Alfred was a pioneering administrator, educator and all-round pen-pusher. One of his major grumbles about the kingdom he ruled for nearly thirty years was that, while it was full of excellent scholarly books, there wasn't anybody left with enough education to read them. Alfred was such a workaholic that he went to the trouble of inventing a new sort of lantern so that he could slave over his paperwork long into the night.

Greatness appears to have run in the family, as Aethelfleda, Alfred's daughter and the 'Lady of the Mercians', was pretty great too. A fine strategist and keen fortress-builder, she was also the only Anglo-Saxon queen ever to lead her troops into battle (against the Welsh – Aethelfleda delegated the Viking fighting to her brother Edward). In fact, Aethelfleda was pretty much England's last successful and enduring female ruler until Elizabeth I came along in 1558. For the intervening 640 years, it was more or less kings all the way. Now that's what I call a Dark Age.

There must be something about English kings whose names start with 'Ed' and end with 'II' that attracts gruesome bottom-related canards. We'll hear all about Edward II and the red-hot poker in due course – but in the eleventh century it was the death of Edmund II that was the subject of the myth-making.

Edmund died in 1016, probably from wounds sustained in battle against the Danes of Cnut. But pretty soon a grisly rumour started doing the rounds, a rumour that persists to this day: Edmund, it was said, actually died from being stabbed in the bum while on the toilet – or, alternatively, from having an arrow fired up there by a very accurate assassin.

It's not long now until the Normans arrive and spoil everything. But there's still time for the Anglo-Saxons to squeeze in one more notable king: Edward the Confessor (not to be confused with Edward I – we only started numbering our

monarchs after the Normans came along, possibly because it was thought that 'William I' had a more regal ring to it than 'William the Bastard').

Edward the Confessor was the son of Ethelred the Unready (whose nickname, by the way, means that he was 'without advisors' rather than that he was ill-prepared). He was one of England's most tiresomely religious kings, and that's up against some stiff competition indeed, as we shall see. So thoroughly holy was he that he was canonised in 1161. Edward was given the title 'Confessor' instead of 'Saint' because, while he met all the necessary criteria for saintliness, he had fallen at the final hurdle by failing to die horribly for his religion.

Edward's marriage to Edith, daughter of Earl Godwine of Essex, was never consummated – for 'religious reasons'. This was an excuse other monarchs might have done well to take note of. The medieval King Henry of Castile, for instance, also failed to consummate his first marriage – and wound up being remembered by posterity as 'Henry the Impotent'.

The Conquest

or, Stormin' Normans

Ten. Sixty. Six.

It's an iconic date, of course, right up there in the top three most significant sixty-sixes in English history (probably ahead of the Great Fire of London but just behind the World Cup win). It's a date etched on the nation's consciousness far more indelibly than that of, say, the signing of Magna Carta or the execution of Charles I (no, I'm not telling you, you'll have to look it up for yourself).

And with good reason. After all, coming under the Norman yoke must have been a terrific shock to all true and free-born Englishmen and women. They were much more used to being under the Viking yoke. And the Roman yoke. The Norman yoke must have been a yoke too far – but still, having a French king was probably good preparation for all the Scottish, Dutch and German kings who were to make themselves at home here over the next ten centuries or so.

The Norman Conquest began with a complex Anglo-Saxon game of thrones and ended – inasmuch as it ever ended – on a bloody, windswept and corpse-strewn stretch of Sussex countryside.

The death of Edward the Confessor in 1066 started the trouble. Edward – who was, by the way, half-Norman – neglected to name a successor (and, for reasons already established, was childless when he died). There were, as a result, four contenders for his still-warm throne: William the Bastard, Duke of Normandy, who was a great-nephew of Cnut, the Danish ruler of England before the Confessor; Edgar, the 15-year-old

great-nephew of the Confessor himself; Harald Hardrada, the mighty King of Norway and – debatably – Denmark; and Harold Godwinson, Earl of Wessex and the Confessor's brother-in-law.

As we know, it was Godwinson who got the gig, was named Harold II, and wound up dead at Hastings with an arrow in his eye.

Except that he didn't. But we'll come to that in a moment.

The lead-up to the clash at Hastings was marked by bloody death and high farce.

First, Harald Hardrada (Harald-with-an-A) arrived in the North of England, bent on pillage and conquest. He and his men made an awful mess of numerous towns along the North Sea coast. Their patented havoc-wreaking technique was to climb to high ground overlooking the settlement they wanted to trash and light huge bonfires. They would then send flaming logs crashing down on to the homes, workplaces and churches below.

Life was never dull when the Vikings were around.

Harald-with-an-A's advance southward was slowed, finally, when the massed forces of Northumbria and Mercia mustered at York in September to oppose him. They failed. In the marshes of Fulford on 20 September, they were cut to pieces. The slaughter was such that it was said the victorious Norwegians were able to walk 'dry-shod over the marsh on the bodies of the slain'.

So Harald-with-an-A's invasion continued. Down South, Harold-with-an-O, perhaps muttering sourly, 'If you want a job doing properly …', assembled his men, and marched north.

Stamford Bridge (the Yorkshire one, not the Chelsea one) was the setting for the hot Harold-on-Harald action that broke out a week later. It was a fine last hurrah for Harold-with-an-O.

The omens were against Harald from the off. When the two kings faced each other ahead of the battle, the Norwegian, in an unscripted burst of slapstick, fell off his horse. 'I think his luck has left him,' Harold remarked, presumably stifling a giggle.

Harold then started in with the pre-match banter. He offered Harald a tract of English land: 'six feet – or seven feet, as he was taller than other men.' He was, for those not versed in the subtleties of Anglo-Saxon wit, offering the Norwegian king a burial plot.

The Norwegians were not, however, excessively intimidated by Harold. They described him as 'a little man, but [grudgingly added] he sat well in his stirrups'. Better than the pratfalling Harald, anyway.

In the end, after fierce fighting and the loss of perhaps 10,000 men, Little Harold prevailed over Big Harald. The Norwegian casualties were so great that only twenty-four ships (out of a fleet of more than 300) were needed to carry the survivors away. It was said that the bones of the dead whitened the battlefield for a generation afterward.

Among the dead was Harold's brother Tostig who – in one of those touching gestures of fraternal loyalty that have characterised royal families down the ages – had sailed to England as Harald-with-an-A's second in command. Tostig's body was so badly mutilated that he could only be identified by a wart between his shoulder blades.

So the Vikings were vanquished. But Harold couldn't stay around to celebrate; there was news from the south coast. Some French bastard had arrived at Pevensey with an army at his back.

There was a strange and confused sort of prelude to the clash at Hastings. In the late summer of 1066, the English fleet that Harold had sent to patrol the English Channel came across an unknown fleet in the midst of tempestuous weather. Little came of the encounter; the English, probably more concerned with battling the elements, noted that the strange-looking sailors wore their hair cropped short – and assumed they were priests. They were not. They were William's Normans, waiting for the go-ahead to launch their invasion. The English would get a much closer look at them come 14 October.

Omens, William would probably have told you, are what you make of them. The appearance of Halley's Comet in the spring of 1066 was one such; it was widely held to relate in some way to the English succession crisis – but how? In that enigmatic way of omens, the comet was maddeningly non-specific.

The quick-thinking Duke of Normandy famously spun a mishap into a motivational slogan on arrival in England. According to legend, William stumbled and fell on Pevensey beach – surely, his aghast troops must have thought, a pretty terrible omen for the upcoming battle. But unlike poor Harald Hardrada, left floundering in the Yorkshire mud unable to think up a witty retort, William had a zinger ready: taking two fistfuls of Sussex sand, he declared that he had seized his new kingdom with both hands. Hurrahs all round!

The Normans weren't entirely trusting to good fortune, of course. To be doubly sure of victory, they had all promised to give up eating meat on Saturdays if they won.

There was one more mystifying omen still to come before the battle could be decided one way or the other. On the morning of 14 October, William, Duke of Normandy, rose, dressed, took up his 'hauberk' or mail-shirt – and put it on backwards. Fortunately he realised his mistake before taking to the field. Goodness knows what the superstitious Normans would have made of a leader who goes into battle in a back-to-front hauberk.

The Battle of Hastings took place not at Hastings but at Senlac Hill, about 7 miles away (historians subsequently decided that 'Hastings' had a better ring to it, like estate agents who bill a flat in Battersea as being in South Chelsea).

There were a lot of men at Hastings-cum-Senlac (perhaps around 20,000) and not much room. It was said that the English ranks were so tightly packed during the fighting that dead men were unable to fall to the ground.

The Englishmen's main weapons were the battleaxe (a popular Danish import), the javelin, which had a range of about 30 yards, and the 'battle shout', which generally followed the flinging of the javelin and was designed to put the wind right up any Norman who found himself in earshot.

Like any battle, Hastings was a wild confusion of courage, terror, triumph, loss, death and blood. There were many heroes and just as many villains. But few soldiers on either side can have made such a grand contribution to the gaiety of the conflict as the Norman knight Taillefer.

Taillefer, evidently a sort of kamikaze minstrel, broke ranks in the midst of the battle and single-handedly charged the

English army – while strumming his instrument and singing 'The Song of Roland'. As another French soldier was to say in different circumstances some 800 years later: 'It is magnificent, but it is not war.'

The Bastard of Normandy, meanwhile, was in the thick of the fighting. Remarkably, William had three horses killed under him during the battle, marking him out as a seriously lucky general (or possibly as a rider of seriously unlucky horses).

And what of Harold-with-an-O? Well, as we all know, Hastings didn't end well for him. He and his knackered army were no match for William's Normans – and so the Bastard became the Conqueror, and a new era of English history began.

But Harold II did not, it seems, meet his death at the business end of a Norman arrow. The evidence we have suggests that,

instead, he was cut down by a troop of Norman knights – and that was hardly the worst of it (though Harold himself might have disagreed). After he had fallen, one of the knights mutilated his corpse so horribly – history has spared us the ghastly details – that William had him drummed out of the army.

Thus the Norman age began. There would be plenty more bloodshed before it was done.

William was crowned King of England on Christmas Day, 1066. Job done? Not quite. There was one more enemy force to be crushed before William's conquest was complete. Harold was dead, and his Wessex-men a spent force. Vikings, then? No: there were coastal raids by Danes and Norwegians in the late summer of 1069, but a few sacks of Norman gold were enough to buy peace and send the longboats home.

The Conqueror reserved his fiercest assault not for any foreign power but for his own subjects. In particular, he went after the northerners. Rebellions across the north and west had, by the start of 1070, exhausted William's patience. It was time for a reckoning.

No one saw it coming. In February, the Normans surged north, sweeping through Yorkshire and closing in on 'St Cuthbert's land', the far north-east that had been Northumbria's rebel heartland. The Conqueror's soldiers rampaged as far north as the Tyne, taking no prisoners, giving no quarter, and showing no mercy. Jarrow church was burned to the ground. The rebels fled; William ordered his men to hunt them down.

The viciousness of William's assault appalled even his Norman followers. Heading south from a burnt-out Tyneside, the king led his men over the bleak, boggy Pennines (a march of inhumane harshness, during which his men were reduced to eating the flesh of their own drowned horses) to savagely put down a rising in Chester. Norman troops ran wild in Shropshire, Staffordshire and Derbyshire, spreading ruin and starvation.

What followed became known as 'The Harrying of the North'. Within a year, William had reduced more than 100 square miles of his own kingdom to a bleak, windswept wilderness. Orderic Vitalis wrote:

He [the Conqueror] harried the land and burnt homes to ashes ... Nowhere else had William shown such cruelty. In his anger he commanded that all crops and herds, chattels and food of every kind, should be brought together and burned to ashes with consuming fire, so that the whole region north of the Humber might be stripped of all means of sustenance. In consequence, so serious a scarcity was felt in England, and so terrible a famine fell upon the humble and defenceless populace, that more than 100,000 Christian folk of both sexes, young and old, perished of hunger.

In 1086, sixteen years after the horrors of the Harrying, Domesday Book set down in writing the value of the towns and villages of England. In the section dedicated to the north, estate after estate is summed up in a single word: waste.

The Middle Ages

or, How We Learned to Stop Worrying and Love the French

Now that Willy I has been dealt with, we can press on with the rest of the old schoolboy's rhyme for remembering the order of England's monarchs:

Willy, Willy, Harry, Ste;
Harry, Rick, John, Harry Three;
One, two, three Neds, Richard Two;
Harries Four, Five, Six, then who?

Edwards four, five, Dick the bad;
Harries twain, and Ned the Lad …

And we can dispose of the lot of them – a panoply of kings (and they are all kings) stretching from the Conqueror's death in 1087 to the sixteenth-century reign of 'the lad' Edward VI – under one sweeping and helpfully vague heading: the Middle Ages.

William 'Rufus', the Conqueror's son, soon made it clear that he intended to be no more indulgent towards misbehaving northerners than his father had been in the long winter of 1070. In 1095, William acted decisively to quash a rebellion led by Robert de Mowbray, the Earl of Northumbria. De Mowbray got off surprisingly lightly, with a sentence of life imprisonment. One of his fellow rebel leaders got off less lightly: he was blinded and castrated. Another was whipped in every church in Salisbury – and then hanged.

But William's reign wasn't all about death and destruction. There was illegal sex, too.

Anselm, the maddeningly pious Archbishop of Canterbury, was much exercised about such issues. In February 1094, while William waited impatiently at Hastings for a favourable wind to carry him to Normandy, Anselm pestered the king to let him hold a general council of the Church in order to attack the crimes of sodomy and incest which, he believed, had become rife throughout the kingdom. This led to a furious row (more about administration of the abbeys than about sodomy), but Anselm eventually got his way: in 1102, a full-scale council of bishops and abbots met to discuss such issues as monks' tonsures, secret marriages, and the wearing of long hair. And, yes, sodomy.

They concluded that, on the whole, they were against it.

In 1100 Henry I, the fourth son of William I, took a bold step towards reconciling the ruling Norman elite with the Anglo-Saxon citizenry the Conqueror had, well, conquered, when he married Edith, the niece of Edgar Aetheling and a descendant of Edward the Confessor.

HENRY I

And a fat lot of good it did him. The aforementioned ruling Norman elite sneeringly referred to the royal couple by the cod-Anglo-Saxon names 'Godric and Godgifu'.

His brother Robert, meanwhile, who would be a thorn in the side of the English king for years to come, was somewhat vertically challenged – and went through life with the insensitive nickname 'Curt-hose' ('shorty-pants') as a result.

England's destiny was thrown into turmoil in 1120 when the *White Ship* sank in the North Sea. One of the 300 souls lost was William Adelin, King Henry's son – his only legitimate heir.

It was, as the rhyme says, King Ste(phen) – Henry's nephew – who would eventually succeed the king, and in doing so plunge the country into civil war as he battled for the throne with Matilda, Henry's daughter. But we might instead have had an undisputed Empress Matilda (and our first post-Norman queen some 400 years early) had Stephen been a less cautious man. Stephen, then plain Stephen of Blois, had been about to board the doomed *White Ship* with William in 1120. But he decided against it at the last minute – because he noticed that the crew were all drunk.

If the sinking of the *White Ship* gave boozing a bad name, the death of Henry in 1135 did the same for feasting – or at least, for feasting on lampreys.

Henry's doctor had expressly forbidden him to eat lampreys, but, while on a hunting trip, he feasted on them anyway – and died as a result. His death has legendarily been attributed to a 'surfeit of lampreys', but modern historians maintain that

Henry did not overindulge in lampreys, he just ate lampreys in contravention of his doctor's advice.

Lampreys are primitive, slimy, jawless fish that attach themselves to bigger fish and suck their blood. They are essentially ocean-going leeches. It could be said that anyone deliberately eating them deserves everything they get.

The decades that followed the reigns of Henry and Stephen were the heyday of the Plantagenets. When Henry II – the grandson of Henry I – came to the throne in 1154, he initiated a royal line that will take us all the way up to the second verse and Dick the Bad.

The grand name of 'Plantagenet' derives from a rather workaday origin. Geoffrey of Anjou, Henry II's dad and the founder of the dynasty, was in the habit of wearing a jolly sprig of broom flower in his hat – which had the Latin name *Planta genista*.

According to legend, the family's ancient origins were yet more curious. The Plantagenets liked to tell the tale of their early ancestor, a Count of Anjou, who married a woman called Mefusive. She turned out to be a witch – and, when the count asked her to attend Mass, she vanished in a puff of smoke.

Just the sort of family you'd want running your country.

One of the defining episodes of Henry II's reign came in 1170, when the pain-in-the-bum Archbishop of Canterbury, Thomas Becket, was murdered in Canterbury Cathedral.

The famously ambiguous *cri de coeur* made by Henry prior to the murder – 'Who will rid me of this turbulent priest?!' – is a classic example of historical misquotation. According to the best

evidence we have, what the exasperated king actually said was less snappy and more, well, abusive. That statement in full:

> What miserable drones and traitors have I nourished in my household, who let their lord be treated with such shameful contempt by a low-born clerk!?

In any case, the result was the same: the archbishop's brains strewn across the cathedral floor.

The notoriously promiscuous William the Conqueror set something of a trend for out-of-wedlock fathering among the kings that succeeded him. Henry II, for instance, had twelve illegitimate children, eight of whom were by a woman named Ikenai, described in some chronicles as 'a common prostitute'.

Henry's son John was just as prolific. John also fathered twelve children outside his marriage – and yet somehow still ended up with the derisive nickname 'Softsword' …

Robin Hood didn't exist. Sorry.

Richard I – son of Henry, brother of John – also had a keen interest in extracurricular activities. In his case, however, these were generally of the crusading rather than carnal variety. He was much more interested in crusading than in the dreary business of ruling; in the course of his ten-year reign, 'the Lionheart' spent just ten months in England.

His antipathy towards 'his' country makes some sense when one considers that Richard was basically French. Practically everybody was French in the eleventh century. He once remarked, 'I would sell London if I could find a buyer.'

Even illness couldn't keep Richard from his beloved Crusades. In 1191, he directed manoeuvres at the Siege of Acre during the Third Crusade, despite suffering from 'arnaldia', a disease that caused all his hair and fingernails to fall out.

In fairness, not all of Richard's holidays abroad were entirely voluntary. On one occasion he enjoyed an extended stay on the Continent as a result of being imprisoned by the Archduke of Austria – after throwing his country's flag into a privy.

His reputation remained fearsome in England even while his person was behind bars, though. One royal official in Cornwall, who had taken advantage of Richard's imprisonment to plot against him, heard that the king was coming home – and promptly died of fright.

RICHARD, I.

Richard remained overseas even after his death in 1199. He was buried in France – specifically, and impressively, in three different parts of France. His heart was interred in Rouen, his body in Anjou, and his entrails in Châlus, where he had died.

To make up for Robin Hood not existing, we can instead take a look at an eleventh-century outlaw who came back from the Crusades and started causing trouble on behalf of the common folk. He was not Robin Hood – repeat, Robin Hood did not exist. He was William Beard.

His actual name was William FitzOsbert, but he did have an outstandingly well-cultivated beard, either as a protest against clean-shaven Norman chins or as a way of standing out from the crowd (it's all very well representing the common man, but one doesn't necessarily want to look like him).

William Beard's rebellion ended, unsurprisingly, with him being horribly killed. He was tied to a horse and dragged through London before being hanged in chains. Fragments of the chain were preserved by some as religious relics.

Not everyone who visited twelfth-century London had as bad a time as poor William. In 1170, for instance, the chronicler William Fitzstephen thought it rather splendid – the only inconveniences being 'the immoderate drinking of fools and the frequent fires'.

'King John was not a good man', A.A. Milne tells us in his famous poem 'King John's Christmas' (which carries on with a lot of nonsense about a big, red India-rubber ball). In real life, well, King John was not a good man, but he did sign Magna Carta in 1215.

Magna Carta is often held up as a grand charter promising freedom from tyranny for the common folk of England, which it sort of was – but, more importantly to the barons who forced John to sign it, it was also a way of protecting England's

rich nobles from being repeatedly stiffed by their avaricious monarch. One historian has described Magna Carta as having 'all the glamour of an appeal against an assessment by the Inland Revenue'.

Magna Carta didn't get rave reviews from everybody. The Pope, for instance, wasn't a fan. He said that it was 'null and void of all validity forever'.

Magna Carta might not have happened at all if John's eyes hadn't been bigger than his tummy.

It's true that John signed the historic charter (at the meadow called Runnymede in Surrey – an acre of which was donated to the US in 1965 as a memorial to John F. Kennedy, and is now officially American soil – although you don't need a passport to visit it). But he wasn't remotely happy about it.

In October 1216, the probability was that England would be invaded by France and, under Prince Louis, Magna Carta would be forgotten about. Alternatively, John might have defeated the French and the rebel barons, and Magna Carta would be forgotten about.

A third option was that King John would eat an ill-advisedly enormous supper, die from a horrendous bout of diarrhoea, and be succeeded by his young son Henry, under whom Magna Carta would be clasped to the royal bosom. Which is exactly what did happen. Hurrah!

Henry III, John's son and the ruler of England for fifty-six years in the thirteenth century, was much more of a stay-at-home monarch than his father and uncle. He was known for his devout godliness – but he also knew how to throw a party.

For his Christmas feast in 1251, for instance, he put out an order for swans from across England: 351 – around 3 tonnes of swan – were served up.

In February, 1236, the River Thames burst its banks. The flood waters, in an appalling show of disrespect, had the temerity to enter the Grand Palace at Westminster. 'Small boats could float there,' one chronicler wrote, 'and people went to their apartments on horseback.'

Hopefully such a calamity will never befall modern-day Westminster. Imagine the expenses claims.

The thirteenth century as a whole is generally remembered by students of English history as being 'pretty boring', briefly enlivened by John's battle with the barons but otherwise a 100-year-long non-event. But this was, in fact, a century of key turning points, real historical water-cooler moments.

For one thing, England was very nearly taken over by France (yes, again). If it hadn't been for a decisive English victory at Lincoln in 1217 – admittedly a victory so easy it became known as 'Lincoln Fair' – England might today be a French dominion, like (but not very like) Martinique or Guadeloupe.

For another thing, this was the century in which Parliament was invented. Yes, the first 'parliament' (the term was coined from the French in 1235) was basically just the king having a chat with some aristocrats about current affairs – but, as the century proceeded and rebel nobles (most notably the religious fanatic Simon de Montfort) started making inroads into royal authority, the modern concept of a parliament began – very gradually – to take shape.[2]

Kings tend not to be grateful to those who pioneer democracy. Simon de Montfort was killed in battle and messily dismembered in 1265. He later had a university in Leicester named after him; whether or not that makes up for him having his head cut off and decorated with his own severed testicles is a moot point.

The fourteenth century was an unutterably horrible century in which to have to live. It was one of those centuries in which the Four Horsemen of the Apocalypse really earned their keep.

First came the famine. Poor harvests and endless rain between 1315 and 1317 caused such devastating scarcity that in some areas of England as many as one in ten villagers died of starvation. In big towns like London, people were reduced to eating dogs.

War, of course, was pretty much a given. If it wasn't Edward I fighting the Scots (and the Scots fighting for their FREEDOOMMMMM), it was Edward II fighting the French. Or Edward III fighting the French. Or Edward II fighting the Scots. Anyway. Wars? We got 'em.

(A quick mention for one of the century's more colourful skirmishes, the 1346 Battle of Neville's Cross. This clash of the English and Scottish armies was overseen, bizarrely, by a chorus of singing monks from Durham. Afterwards, King David II of Scotland was found under a bridge by a yeoman called John Copeland. David punched out his teeth.)

Then came The Pestilence. Not just a pestilence, The Pestilence – the Black Death, the great scourge, 'the Mortality'. The highest-profile English victim of this horrendous plague wasn't even in England when the Black Death caught up with her: Princess Joan, the daughter of Edward III, had been sent to the Continent to marry Pedro of Castile just weeks before.

She succumbed to the pestilence in Bordeaux in August. She was 13 years old.

In a letter to King Alfonso, Pedro's father, Edward wrote:

See, with what intense bitterness of heart we have to tell you this, destructive Death (who seizes young and old alike, sparing no one and reducing rich and poor to the same level) has lamentably snatched from both of us our dearest daughter, whom we loved best of all, as her virtues demanded.

This was a bitter foretaste of what was to come once the plague took hold in England. The Black Death made landfall at Melcombe in Devon on 23 June – Midsummer's Eve – 1348. It didn't leave until around 1½ million people lay dead.

It also had a significant impact on haute couture. Let me explain.

Like most plagues, the Black Death was a pauper's plague, a class-conscious pestilence that preferred to wreak havoc in slums and prisons than bother the lords of England's manors; 'This sickness befell people everywhere,' one chronicler noted, 'but especially the middling and lower classes, rarely the great.'

As the plague did its ghastly work and the population perished in their thousands, it became clear to the lords and landowners that prompt, effective action had to be taken. In every parish in the land, working people were suffering horrible deaths. The dead lay unburied – for there was no one left to bury them – and grass grew in the marketplaces. In London, Edward III ordered that the streets be cleared of corpses, only to be told that all the street cleaners had died from the plague. If this tragic state of affairs were allowed to continue, the aristocracy foresaw a truly horrifying consequence: wages were going to go up.

So, as the Black Death raged all about them, England's lawmakers passed legislation designed to protect employers from being left out of pocket by plague-related labour shortages.

The Ordinances of Labourers (1349) were the economic equivalent of putting your fingers in your ears and shouting 'la-la-la, can't hear you' – and, unsurprisingly, they didn't work. People kept dying. Wages kept rising. Increasingly, working people fell into one of two camps: those who were getting richer, and those who were dead.

Soon, the Establishment's worst fears were realised. The middle-classes started getting uppity. They finally had a bit of brass in their pockets – and they wanted people to know it. One way of flashing the cash in medieval England was to dress in fine clothes. Fashions that had been the exclusive preserve of aristocrats and other poshos were soon being sported by mere merchants, for goodness' sake. The entire social order was trembling. This would not stand. The Establishment cracked down hard.

The Sumptuary Laws of 1363 are among the most preposterous ordinances ever passed by an English parliament. They were essentially the law's answer to the aristocrat's plea: 'If just anyone can wear 24in winklepickers, how will people know I'm an aristocrat?' Under the law, merchants were forbidden to wear pointy shoes in excess of 6.½in in length. A gentleman's pointy shoes might lawfully extend to 12in. The right to wear shoes measuring a magnificent 2ft in length was granted only to the nobility. The law also forbade handicraftsmen's wives to wear silk veils and prohibited the wearing of velvet by the daughters of knight-bachelors.

Thus was the God-given social order of England maintained.

Edward III, meanwhile, didn't catch the plague, but he was subject to bouts of dysentery. On one occasion he was prescribed a 'medicinal' paste of ambergris, musk, pearls, gold and silver, at a cost of £134 – the yearly income of three knights.

The 1300s also saw England's domestic politics descend to a level of eye-watering brutality. The deposition and (probable) murder of Edward II is a case in point. Whether or not the stories about his 1327 death by red-hot-poker-to-the-lower-bowel are true, it's certainly the case that his key ally in his later years, Hugh Despenser the Younger, was executed in a staggeringly savage way.

At Shrewsbury, in 1326, Despenser was stripped and crowned with stinging nettles. Biblical verses were scrawled on his skin. Condemned to death as a traitor, he was hanged from a height of 50ft; still alive, he was cut down and disembowelled, before finally being beheaded. His head was displayed on London Bridge and the dismembered pieces of his body were sent to

Bristol, Dover, York, and Newcastle. All of this was done at the behest of the unofficial Regent, Roger Mortimer, and his lover Isabella – Edward II's wife.

But let's take a moment to reflect on happier moments in the rein of Edward II – such as the many jovial hours he spent watching his personal 'tumbler' repeatedly fall off his horse, for 20s a tumble. Good times. Or the occasion on which he marked the anniversary of the murder of his friend Piers Gaveston by going to France and taking in a show – of twenty naked dancers.

This was a king who deserves to be remembered for more than ending up on the wrong end of Roger Mortimer's fire irons.

In any case, Edward II's grisly end wasn't even the most gruesome event of the fourteenth century. That title goes to the Peasants' Revolt.

Many people nowadays think that the Peasants' Revolt of 1381 was simply a matter of robust Kentish hayseeds sticking up for their rights in the face of a beastly king. They're sort of right. But they're also sort of wrong.

The monarchy of England wasn't in its best possible shape when the revolt broke out in 1381. The king, Richard II, was a 14-year-old boy. His reign had begun in 1377 with a coronation ceremony of ludicrous splendour: the new king was showered with flakes of gold, and, in parts of London, the water pipes ran with wine. But the party soon petered out.

The power behind the throne was John of Gaunt, Richard's uncle and a supremely haughty (and hated) aristocrat's aristocrat. The 1377 heresy trial of John Wyclif showcased John's unique brand of charm; as the debate grew heated, he threatened to drag the Bishop of London to Windsor by his hair.

The rebels of south-east England – whose grievances stemmed from (a) heavy taxation and (b) obnoxious tax collectors – stormed London in June 1381. One of their foremost targets was the Savoy Palace, the lavish residence of John of Gaunt.

Thirty of the rebels got lucky: they discovered the entrance to John's wine cellar. Plundering was against the 'rules' set out by Wat Tyler, the legendary leader of the revolt and the most influential roofer in history – but the booze-stash of England's grandest noble was too much to resist. In the cellar, corks popped and fine wine flowed. Above ground, meanwhile, the air was filled with smoke, dust and the noises of destruction as the palace was reduced to a ruin – and the entrance to the cellar was blocked off. We don't know whether it was suffocation or starvation that got the revellers in the end. All we know is that within a fortnight, all thirty of them were dead.

After that, things started to get really gruesome.

At Bury St Edmunds in Suffolk, the rebels executed Sir John Cavendish and John of Cambridge – and used their severed heads as puppets in a puppet show. In London, as the revolt approached its climax and Tyler struck at the very heart of power, the Archbishop of Canterbury, Simon Sudbury, found himself with his head on the executioner's block. The executioner, however, was hardly a credit to his profession. It took him eight hacks to sever the archbishop's head. Once it had been removed, the head – complete with its mitre – was paraded through London on a pole. Why didn't the mitre fall off? Why, because the merry peasants had nailed it in place.

The revolt, like most revolts, eventually lost its momentum and was then brutally suppressed by the authorities. Richard II continued to rule. Things went back to normal, and it was nearly a whole year before the next deeply disturbing thing happened.

In May 1382, the people of London and the south-east were thrown into panic – yes, again – by, of all things, an earthquake. In London, the cathedrals of Westminster and St Paul's were severely rattled; Christ Church in Canterbury sustained damage, as did All Saints' church in Hollingbourne, Kent. At Blackfriars, a council convened to examine the Lollards for heresy was interrupted by the tremors – it was subsequently known as 'the Council of the Earthquake'.

The most serious damage was done not to the country's buildings but to the fragile psyches of its people. Those who had survived famine, war, plague, revolt and earthquake must have wondered if anyone would make it out of the century alive.

When people in fourteenth-century London did find ways to have a good time, other people had the brass neck to complain about it – people like Bishop Braybrooke, who in 1385 moaned that people were shooting birds in the gardens of Saint Paul's Cathedral – and, even worse, 'playing ball' in the nave.

If Bishop Braybrooke thought that was disrespectful, it's to be hoped he was never aware of what happened in the cathedral a few hundred years later – to his own preserved corpse. After the Great Fire of 1666 and the subsequent rebuilding of St Paul's, Braybrooke's body was put on display and became an object of admiration and veneration.

The Countess of Oxford, better known as the raffish actress Hester Davenport, took the opportunity to bite off the bishop's genitals.

Richard II, forced to abdicate and banged up in a Yorkshire prison, died in 1400. His end – like that of many a deposed king – was murky; it's thought that (contra Shakespeare, who had him battling hand-to-hand with the villainous Sir Piers Exton), he starved to death in his jail cell, but we don't know for sure. It was a dismal end to a dismal century.

Come the 1400s, come the Henrys. Things could only get better.

Henry IV was one of England's great beardies. Even centuries after his death, his beard was impressive: when his tomb was opened in 1832, it was found to be 'thick and matted, and of a deep russet colour'.

Henry went into a sort of semi-retirement in later life as a result of ill-health. It was whispered about the kingdom that he had been struck down with leprosy for executing the rebellious archbishop, Richard Scrope.

As we've seen, the old comic poem about King 'Arold with an eyeful of arrow (on his 'orse with his 'awk in his 'and) might not, after all, have been strictly haccurate. But there was one English king who certainly did receive an arrow in the general vicinity of his eye – and this one proved rather more effective at seeing off the French.

Henry V, thanks to good press from PR man Mr W. Shakespeare, holds a privileged place in our national history. He was, it's true, the hero of Agincourt. He was also a crashingly dull religious fundamentalist (rather like Richard I, he was able to combine crusading Christianity with a penchant for butchering prisoners of war).

He was merely Prince Henry when, battling Henry Percy's revolting Welsh at Shrewsbury in 1403, he sustained the wound. Shrewsbury was the first battle fought on English soil in which two armies of longbowmen faced each other. It was a fearsome clash: 2,000 men saw sense and deserted even before it began, and, once it did, scores of men were sliced to pieces by the whistling clouds of arrows. It would have impressed on the 17-year-old Prince Hal the unsurpassed military might of the English longbow.

And he got a close-up view of this fearsome weapon when, fighting in the midst of the battle, an arrow struck him just beneath his right eye, penetrating the bone to a depth of 6in. Henry refused to leave the field until the battle was won.

Twelve years later, Henry was leading the English army at Agincourt – a battle that might never have happened without a little help from pantomime's best-loved Lord Mayor of London.

In 1415, Richard 'Dick' Whittington was a successful merchant and man-about-town with a lucrative sideline in moneylending. When King Henry came to the City cap-in-hand, talking of a new mission to reconquer the (French) possessions of the throne, Whittington dug deep – the £700 he donated was a major boost to the war effort.

Henry's money-grubbing was shameless even by royal standards. He had already secured a loan of 800 marks from the people of Norfolk by pawning the jewel-studded crown of Richard II, the king usurped by his father, Henry IV.

Dick's largesse didn't necessarily mean that the English army travelled to France in high style. Napoleon might have believed that 'an army marches on its stomach' – but the English longbowmen who would later be feted as the heroes of Agincourt were so short of rations that, on the way to the battle, they were forced to forage in the countryside for nuts and berries.

The English longbow was at the bleeding edge (quite literally) of medieval military technology. Yew wood – hard, but elastic – was the favoured material for the 6ft bow.

But just how English were these 'English' longbows? Arthur Conan Doyle, in his 1891 'Song of the Bow', wrote the following:

the bow was made in England
Of true wood, of yew wood
The wood of English bows

The reality, though, is that English yews couldn't supply the volume of timber needed to keep the army equipped. The yew stands of Britain and Ireland were soon exhausted; England began to import yew wood from Spain and, then, from the towns of the North and Baltic seas. This medieval arms trade soon assumed a vast scale: huge amounts of yew wood came from the Alpine borders, and Polish tradesmen in Danzig received bargeloads of yew from the deep woods of Eastern Europe.

During the first half of the sixteenth century, Bavaria and Austria alone exported around a million yew staves; by 1568,

there wasn't a single yew left in Bavaria. This wasn't a cottage industry of homely, simple-minded bowyers and fletchers; this was the military-industrial complex at work.

The longbow was not, however, the first military application of strong-but-stretchy yew wood. Its use in weaponry goes back much further – almost as far back as our old friend Roger de Boxgrove. A sharpened point of yew wood, carefully honed and seasoned in a fire, was found at Clacton-on-Sea in Essex in 1911 – and is believed to be 400,000 years old. It's one of the most ancient wooden artefacts ever discovered, and was probably used as a spear.

The longbows used at Agincourt had a range of perhaps 300 yards – quite an improvement on the javelins of Hastings – and a skilled archer could loose an arrow every ten seconds. Henry's army had around 5,000 skilled archers. That's a lot of arrows.

The battle itself was, of course, a bloody and miserable business. The most notorious deaths at Agincourt were those of the dozens – perhaps hundreds – of French prisoners murdered by the English archers on the orders of their king.

There was some reluctance among the archers to do away with their POWs in cold blood – mainly because the archers had their eyes on the hefty ransoms they hoped to exact. Henry's archers stood outside the chivalric code that – to a greater or lesser extent – governed the conduct of their more aristocratic comrades in arms. They were, in short, rough old boys; many had only signed up in order to escape punishment for violent crimes (murder included) back home.

If the deaths of the prisoners were the most atrocious at Agincourt, the prize for the most horrible probably has to go to Edward of Langley, 2nd Duke of York. Edward suffocated to death beneath a heap of French corpses.

Henry V himself died in France in 1422. He was the first king to die overseas since Richard I perished from gangrene at Châlus in 1199. Henry never saw his only son – his nine-month-old heir, the future Henry VI.

Henry V's wife (and the other Henry's mother), Catherine of Valois, may have had rather a bore for a husband when she was alive – but, once she was dead, she received some amorous attention from a decidedly roguish character.

In February 1669, the noted diarist, ogler and groper Samuel Pepys arrived at Westminster Abbey with some friends. It was his birthday, so, as a treat, he took a look at Catherine's preserved 268-year-old corpse. Then, as an extra-special treat, he gave her a kiss. 'I had the upper part of her body in my hands, and I did kiss her mouth,' he wrote. 'This was my birth-day, 36 years old [and the day] I did first kiss a Queen.'

One of the most memorable events of Henry VI's troubled reign was the 1450 assault on London by the rebel forces of the outlaw Jack Cade. Nobody really knows much about Cade. Some said he was the alter ego of the physician John Aylmere, who was known for going about dressed all in scarlet. Others said that he was a former soldier and a murderer who dabbled in sorcery. In the summer of 1450, what most people said about him was, 'Aaargh, Jack Cade's coming, run!', because Jack Cade, the Captain of Kent, brought to London chaos and mayhem on a scale not seen since the Peasants' Revolt sixty-nine years before.

Cade and his 25,000 rebels entered London in July. As is traditional in these circumstances, Cade proclaimed that anyone caught looting would be put to death. As is also traditional in these circumstances, everybody ignored the proclamation and promptly set about looting, pillaging, burning and killing. Cade couldn't do much about it, in any case – he was too busy looting.

Henry's grandfather was Charles VI of France, who suffered terribly from hereditary mental illness (at various times believing himself to be St George, refusing to change his clothes or wash for five months, and labouring under the delusion that he was made of glass). Charles had attracted the nickname 'Charles the Mad' pretty early on in his reign. It might not have come as a complete surprise to many when, in the summer of 1453, Henry VI suffered a severe mental breakdown. A state of frenzy was followed by physical collapse and a seventeen-month stupor. It seemed, one chronicler wrote, that 'his wit and reson [were] withdrawen'.

Henry recovered, eventually, but he was a listless and unhappy king for the remainder of his rule – which did not end well. He was executed in May 1471, and his body was left overnight to bleed on the pavement outside St Paul's. 'No king who loses his crown and dies in prison, and whose reign ends in civil war, can be counted a success,' one historian has wisely noted.

Before we move on to the misery of the Wars of the Roses, let's remind ourselves once more that, in between outbreaks of vicious bloodshed, these medieval types really knew how to throw a good banquet – even if their dishes weren't always appealing to the modern palate.

In 1465, at a feast to celebrate the investment of Lord Neville as Archbishop of York, guests were treated to a menu that included 400 herons. The naturalist W.H. Hudson observed that heron-meat is 'tough and has a NASTY TASTE' – but, on the other hand, a sixteenth-century critic noted that 'Heron is lighter of digestion than a Crane'.

Poor old Henry VI was the last Lancastrian Plantagenet to rule England. After his execution, there was a bit of a family squabble over who should have next go; Margaret of Anjou, Henry's widowed queen, was naturally opposed to the claims of the Duke of York, and, after York's death at Wakefield, of his French-born son, Edward, Earl of March.

It's thought that Edward first dipped his toe in England's internecine hostilities at the first Battle of St Albans in 1455 (a skirmish at which, incidentally, the Earl of Wiltshire deserted the Royal Standard and was described by a commentator as fighting 'mainly with his heels, for he was called the most handsome knight in the land and was afraid of losing his beauty'). In March 1461, the Yorkists declared Edward king. At this point, things started to get a bit out of hand. The result was the most devastating battle you've never heard of – indeed, 'the biggest, bloodiest and longest battle on English soil': Towton.

Let's consider the figures. An immense multitude – perhaps as many as 75,000 men – took to the field at Towton, North Yorkshire, on 29 March 1461. By the day's end, 28,000 were dead. That's twenty-eight thousand. Around 1 per cent of the Anglo-Welsh population. Around 4 per cent of the fighting-age male population. More than were killed on the first day of the Battle of the Somme. And there were no machine guns here; this slaughter was achieved by the longbow, the sword, the poleaxe, the mace, and the horseman's hammer.

Of the dead, a staggering 20,000 were men of the House of Lancaster.

Edward IV was, at 6ft 4in, the tallest monarch in English history (though if things had turned out differently, Harald Hardrada might have given him a run for his money). He was a general and a leader of men – and at Mortimer's Cross in February 1461, his first great victory, he showed a flair for improvisation that might have impressed William of Normandy.

On the morning of the battle, the assembled troops beheld an omen in the heavens: three suns appeared to be shining in the sky over the frosty Welsh Marches. To us, it's an optical illusion known as a 'parhelion'. To them – well, who knew what it might signify? Edward knew. The three suns, he declared, thinking quickly, represented the blessing of the Holy Trinity upon another trinity – himself, of course, and his brothers George and Richard (later Richard III, who, in Shakespeare at least, built on the metaphor, describing his brother as 'this sun of York').

The extemporised explanation seemed to do the trick. The Lancastrians were duly routed. But no one likes being routed. That sort of thing creates bad blood. And so to Towton.

Forget all that stuff about Yorkshire-Lancashire rivalry. The Wars of the Roses weren't a cross-Pennine clash; rather, they were a matter of North versus South. The Yorkists were mainly men from south of the River Trent, the Lancastrians mostly from north of it. Each regarded the other as pretty much an alien race (*plus ça change*); the Lancastrians, for instance, found the Kentish Yorkists' habit of drinking beer rather than ale highly suspicious.

Wartime propaganda, coupled with a slew of nasty skirmishes in the eighteen months leading up to Towton, saw to it that this mutual hostility was soon whipped up to fever pitch. When the reckoning came, no quarter would be given.

It was a sleety, cold, miserable Palm Sunday that saw the two forces face off across the Towton field. The Lancastrians had more men, a better position, and home advantage; they hadn't had to march hundreds of miles just to get to the battlefield. But they did have fierce, stinging, blinding sleet blowing into their faces. This puts you at a disadvantage when the opposition archers are re-enacting Agincourt and their arrow-storms are darkening the sky.

The fighting dragged on from daybreak to dusk – when faced with an unbreakable Yorkist line and, what was more, the arrival of Yorkist reinforcements, the Lancastrians cracked. They turned and ran – only to realise that there was nowhere to run to. Uphill was open country, or killing-ground; downhill was the mud of Towton Dale and the turbid waters of the River Cock.

The Lancastrians had themselves destroyed the bridge over the river in order to prevent a Yorkist escape. As the fleeing men piled, dead, dying or soon to be drowned, into the river, a new bridge began to rise from the waters – a 'bridge of bodies'.

Edward had dispatched his men in pursuit of the terrified Lancastrians with the grim order, 'No quarter'. For hundreds of years, the grisly details of the ensuing slaughter were left to our imaginations (or perhaps our nightmares). A chance discovery changed all that.

In 1996, builders working a short distance from the Towton field uncovered a mass grave. The skulls of the forty-three skeletons within were smashed and distorted, the broken bones evidence of a frenzy of savage blows. Studies by scientists at the University of Bradford gave a fuller – and more terrible – picture:

> Many of the individuals suffered multiple injuries that are far in excess of those necessary to cause disability and death. From the distribution of cuts, chops, incisions, and punctures, it appears that blows cluster in the craniofacial area, in some cases bisecting the face and cranial vault of some individuals and detaching bone in others. Series of cuts and incisions found in the vicinity of the nasal and aural areas appear to have been directed toward removal of the nose and ears.

And so on. You don't have to be an anatomist to see that this is a brutal testament to what can be achieved by sword, mace and hammer – plus unthinking hatred, blind rage and unholy terror.

And now for something completely different.

Edward IV, now established on the throne, turned out to be a sort of proto-Henry VIII, a big-eating, big-boozing, big-spending womaniser (though never a ladykiller in the Henry VIII sense). Thomas More noted that in his youth he was 'greatly given to fleshy wantoness'; he scandalised Europe in 1464 by making a secret marriage to the Lancastrian widow Elizabeth Woodville, mainly because he was desperate to have sex with her, and during the rest of his reign carried on with three mistresses – said by More to be 'the merriest, the wiliest, and the holiest in the realm'.

When Edward passed on in 1483, the causes were pretty self-evident. It wasn't the done thing for chroniclers to say that the king had died because he ate like a pig and drank like a fish – but that doesn't mean it wasn't true.

Now, back to the bloodshed.

We only have one more Edward to squeeze in before we get to Dick the Bad, and that won't take long because this Edward, the fifth one, didn't live long – thanks, we think, to his uncle, Dick the Bad (or, more correctly, Richard, Duke of Gloucester).

Edward was 12 when his father Edward IV died. He was still 12 when he was banged up in the Tower with his little brother, Richard of York, on his uncle's orders. He might

well still have been 12 when he (and his brother) were killed, probably but not definitely on his uncle's orders. Richard, Duke of Gloucester, was crowned king in July 1483.

There's not much more to add to the sad story of the Princes in the Tower. One chronicler wrote that, even before Richard's coronation, men wept openly when they spoke of the lost young king, Edward V. They had good reason.

The Welshman Henry Tudor, claimant to the throne, arrived in England with an army of Scotsmen and Frenchmen (and some Englishmen to make up the numbers) in the summer of 1485. He met Richard III's forces at Bosworth, in the West Midlands. Richard had – in theory – a far larger army, but he'd made the mistake of relying on the support of the powerful Stanley family, who were notorious flip-floppers. When the Stanleys entered the fray on Henry's side, the game was up for Richard. He went to his death in the thick of the fighting, screaming, 'Treason, treason, treason!'

The Tudors

or, Usurp if You Like

Henry Tudor, who became Henry VII in the aftermath of Richard III's death at Bosworth, was quite clearly a usurper whose claim to the throne fell somewhere between 'weak' and 'laughable' – but you can't go through history worrying about things like that, or you'll never get anywhere. Some never forgot it, though: in spite of Shakespeare's hatchet job on Richard's reputation, a thread of stubborn Yorkism persisted in English folk memory. Thus, at Bosworth in 1813, a plaque was put in place to mark the spot where 'King Richard fell fighting gallantly in defence of his realm and his crown against the usurper Henry Tudor'.

One of Henry's first moves was to make a good marriage – to a woman who had a far better claim to the throne than he did. Elizabeth Woodville was the daughter of Edward IV and, confusingly, Elizabeth Woodville. Her name might not be familiar, but you'll know her face: the 'Queen' found in a deck of cards was based on the younger Elizabeth's image.

The beautiful new queen soon found herself being showered with exotic gifts. Among the presents sent to her by well-wishers (and sycophants) were some ornamented devotional girdles and a pair of clavichords that are thought to be the first keyboards ever seen in England.

One of Henry's most prized possessions, meanwhile, was the preserved leg of St George. It was given to him after Elizabeth's

HENRY VII

death by Louis XII of France, who wanted Henry to marry his cousin. Henry didn't much fancy the cousin, thanks, but was very taken with the saintly leg; he carried it through London in a state procession on 22 April 1505.

Henry was genuinely grief-stricken by Elizabeth's death in February 1503. After a few years, though, he was thinking about moving on.

The king was a careful, even obsessive man, and he wasn't prepared to take a step as significant as remarriage without due diligence. The target of his researches was the 25-year-old Joanna of Naples, whose husband had died just weeks into their marriage. In 1505, Henry despatched two envoys to Italy to conduct a thorough audit of the young widow. Among the curious king's instructions were: 'Mark the favour of her visage, whether she be painted or no, whether she be fat or lean, sharp or round' (Answer: 'The favour of her visage is after her stature – of very good compass and amiable, and somewhat round and fat'); 'Mark whether her neck be long or short' (Answer: 'Her neck is comely, not misshapen, nor very short nor very long, but her neck seemeth to be shorter because her breasts be full and somewhat big'); 'Mark her breasts, whether they be big or small' (Answer: 'They be somewhat great and full'); and, crucially, 'Mark whether any hair appear upon her lip' (Answer: 'She hath none').

The marriage, in the end, never went ahead – but some future kings (we're looking at you, Henry VIII and George IV) could have learned a lot from Henry where the acquisition of mail-order brides was concerned.

Throughout his reign, Henry's diligence often spilled over into ruthless avarice. The men he appointed to manage the country's finances were gimlet-eyed and shameless in squeezing money from the king's subjects.

A classic example was the strategy known as 'Morton's Fork' (after Henry's advisor John Morton). As a means of calculating a person's wealth, 'Morton's Fork' had you coming and going: if you spent lavishly and ostentatiously, you were obviously loaded, and would be taxed accordingly; if, however, your lifestyle was parsimonious, then you must have had your money salted away somewhere – and therefore were obviously loaded, and would be taxed accordingly.

As well as being the king's advisor, John Morton was the Archbishop of Canterbury. He was not the only senior churchman to fulfil dual roles under Henry's reign. Richard Fox, the hugely influential Bishop of Winchester, had a profitable sideline as a businessman – he was the owner of the biggest brothels in England.

This wasn't really surprising, as the Church in Tudor England was essentially a massive real-estate business that also dabbled in Christianity. By the mid-1500s, around two-thirds of all the buildings in London – houses of ill-repute not excepted – were owned by 'religious persons'.

Henry VII's reign was bedevilled by pretenders to his throne turning up out of the blue and claiming to be this-or-that long-lost heir. One of the most notorious was a youth named Lambert Simnel, who rocked up in 1487 pretending to be the Earl of Warwick, nephew of Edward IV – and asserting his right to be crowned Edward VI of England. Inconveniently, he had a substantial army of Yorkists with him.

Henry's army met the rebels at Stoke and saw them off pretty promptly. Simnel was captured. Henry, though, chose not to kill him – instead, he put him to work as a spit-turner in the royal kitchens.

The reign of Henry VII was also, of course, the childhood of Henry VIII. Henry was not born to be king; his elder brother Arthur was the heir, and Henry, born five years later, was very much a spare. Arthur's sudden death at the age of 18 changed all that. The succession passed to Henry – as, eventually, would Arthur's young widow, one Katherine of Aragon.

Henry was a precociously accomplished child. In October 1494, at the age of just 3, he rode unassisted through London to Westminster to be knighted by his father.

The precocious child grew into a pious youth. The teenaged Henry carried around with him a 'bede roll' or prayer guide that included a daily recitation; if carried out diligently, it promised the supplicant a total of 52,712 years and 40 days free from purgatory after death.

Such things were serious considerations for a medieval monarch. A few hundred years earlier, the death of Richard I had prompted a Bishop of Rochester to calculate that the Lionheart would spend thirty-three years in purgatory as expiation for his sins, and would eventually ascend to Heaven in March 1232.

Henry's exploits in adult life – marital and otherwise – are the stuff of legend. He had so many wives that schoolchildren had to devise a rhyme to remember their fates, although, in the

HENRY VIII

best traditions of rote schooling, it's mostly wrong. This is the edited version:

DIVORCED	(actually annulled, in 1533, on the grounds that she had been married to Henry's brother – and that the marriage had been consummated)
BEHEADED	(actually declared null and void and beheaded, of which more later)
DIED	(this bit is correct: Jane Seymour died at the age of 28, and more than 1,200 Masses were held for her in London alone)
DIVORCED	(again, actually annulled, and survived Henry by ten years)
BEHEADED	(annulled and beheaded – it wouldn't do to go chopping off a woman's head while you were still married to her)
SURVIVED	(yes, Katherine Parr was the one who finally buried the old swine – and, less than six months later, married again, to the dashing Sir Thomas Seymour)

If that hasn't destroyed your faith in rote learning, the names of these six consorts can be remembered with the acrostic All Boys Should Come Home Please (standing for Katherine of Aragon, Anne Boleyn, Jane Seymour, Anne of Cleves, Katherine Howard, and Katherine Parr).

Anne Boleyn, Henry's ill-fated second wife, is the consort people seem to know most about. Did you know that she had six fingers on one hand? You probably did – but actually she didn't. Did you know that she had a little dog that she called

'Purkoy', from the French *pour quoi* ('why') because it had a constantly puzzled expression? You probably didn't.

Purkoy, like Anne, came to a sad end. He fell out of a window, which is probably better than being beheaded, but not by much.

In 1536, a man named William Bowman was arrested for slandering Anne Boleyn by 'saying that her arse is worm-eaten'. Before long, though, Henry was brooding along similar lines himself. He decided that Anne was committing adultery with his body-servant Henry Norris (because of course, if you were going to commit adultery with a servant, you would choose the one who was responsible for wiping your husband's bottom). And once he'd made up his mind to have Anne executed, he threw himself into the arrangements with disturbing zeal.

Here, Henry's penchant for chivalric fantasy came to the fore. He decided that – in a unique breach of protocol – Anne would be beheaded with a sword, rather than an axe. Swords were just more, y'know, Camelotty.

So it came to pass. Before her death, Anne joked: 'I heard say the executioner was very good, and I have but a little neck.' The executioner was indeed very good – the sword stroke was swift, and Anne's eyes and lips were still moving when her severed head landed in the straw.

Henry wasn't just a homicidal maniac, though – he was also, of course, the very model of a late-medieval sex-god. Or was he? Anne didn't think so – she said that he had 'neither talent nor vigour' in bed.

And of course, the king wasn't averse to dishing out crude personal insults to the women in his life. Famously, Anne of Cleves was sourly dismissed by 48-year-old Henry as 'a Flanders mare' (mainly because, at their first meeting in 1540, she was more interested in watching a bout of bull-baiting in the neighbouring courtyard than in his bullish overtures). It didn't stop there. Henry said that he couldn't consummate his marriage to Anne of Cleves because he 'plainly mistrusted her to be no mayd [i.e. a virgin], by reason of the loseness of her brests', and that 'furthermore he could have none appetite with her to do as a man shuld do with his wife'.

Whereas the 24-year-old Anne, of course, should have been over the moon. A thrice-married middle-aged tyrant with leg ulcers, a swollen foot and a 52in waistline? What a catch!

Henry was fanatically enthusiastic about 'the chivalric arts': jousting, fighting, hunting, waging war, cannons, guns and large-scale violence generally. You'd think that the wound in his foot that troubled him greatly in later life would have been sustained in battle, or in a duel, or at least in besting some poor fellow-knight in the jousting lists.

But it wasn't. Henry did it playing tennis.

The wound meant that he had to wear a single loose-fitting black velvet slipper on his injured foot. Sycophants being what they are, the single loose-fitting black velvet slipper became a must-have fashion garment among Henry's courtiers.

In 1526, Henry VIII set himself up for hundreds of years of ridicule by drawing up the 'Eltham Ordinances', a highly detailed list of his day-to-day requirements – including his daily meals.

If you were wondering how you too could achieve that coveted 52in-waistline look, then the Eltham Ordinances are for you. Henry's appetite for eating wildlife rivalled that of the all-consuming Victorian, William Buckland.

At dinner, the king, it seems, sat down to a repast of beef, venison, carp, mutton and swan (or stork, if the shops were out of swan). Then he had a 'fritter' (with custard). Then he moved on to the second course: pheasant (or bittern), quail (or partridge), lamb (or pigeon), plover (or gull), lark (or rabbit), and more venison. And some jelly. The whole lot would be swilled down with 6 gallons or so of beer, and 5 gallons or so of wine.

Downstairs, meanwhile, the servants dined on bread, beer, beef, and veal. But there was no time for them to sit around digesting this grand feast – they had to get plucking, skinning, boning, butchering, roasting, frying, spicing and baking Henry's supper, which was almost as voluminous as his dinner.

Much of what we know about Henry VIII's affairs comes from his Lord Chancellor, Sir Thomas More. More was a brilliant, witty, gifted and humane man – so of course Henry had his head chopped off. As he climbed the scaffold in July 1535,

More asked to the executioner to give him a hand up — and 'coming down, let me shift for myself'.

More family legend tells that Thomas' head was then stuck on a spike on Westminster Bridge. One day, one of his daughters was sailing beneath. 'That head has lain many a time in my lap,' she sighed. 'Would to God it would fall into my lap as I pass under!' File under 'be careful what you wish for'. According to the legend, her father's decomposing severed head did indeed fall into her lap. It was preserved in a church in Canterbury.

Henry's reign wasn't all about the dinner-table, the jousting-field, the bedchamber and the chopping block (well, it was for Henry, but kings aren't everything). There was, it turned out, a whole wide world out there. There were, for the first time, books, and plenty of them. William Caxton had brought the printing press to England in the 1470s – but even fifty years later the church still considered it dangerous new technology. 'We must root out printing,' warned Bishop Tunstall in the 1520s, 'or printing will root out us.'

Others looked out at England's rapidly expanding horizons and saw a world ripe for plunder. One of the most disturbing stories from this burgeoning golden age of piracy, exploration and trade concerned the not-very-good ship *Minion*. In 1509, the *Minion*, captained by slave trader John Hawkins, returned to England from a long voyage to the Americas.

Hawkins was evidently a poor captain as well as a dismal human being. Of his crew of 400, just thirteen had survived the trip. Those who hadn't died from hunger had died during a stop-off in Spain – from overeating.

Also leading the charge to grab a share of the new world being opened up by the pirates, merchants and navies of sixteenth-century Europe was a man of the bluest royal blood. Possibly.

Thomas Stucley was an adventurer. Arrested for piracy in 1558, he was acquitted due to 'lack of evidence' – or, more likely, because it was rumoured that he was Henry VIII's 'base-born son'. The fact that the rumours were probably started by Stucley is neither here nor there. He went on to defraud his own family, so perhaps there was a little bit of Henry in the young rogue after all.

Claiming to be Henry VIII's secret love child was certainly worth a shot. You wouldn't, after all, be the only one. Although Henry was no match in this field for, say, Henry II or John – each of whom could have fielded an entire backstairs football team – he was suspected to have at least seven illegitimate children.

The only one of these to be acknowledged by the king was Henry Fitzroy, Duke of Richmond and Somerset. Fitzroy has the distinction of being listed in the Oxford Dictionary of National Biography as 'Royal Bastard'.

The rules on illegitimacy were transparent and sensible. For example, the future queens Mary and Elizabeth were both born of Henry's annulled marriages (to Katherine of Aragon and Anne Boleyn respectively), and so were both definitely illegitimate, until everybody decided that they weren't.

The reign of Edward VI – 10 years old when he came to the throne, and 'Ned the Lad' in our monarchical mnemonic – was followed by that of Lady Jane Grey, a member of the exclusive club of what we might call Sort-of Monarchs. Four kings and queens of England were never crowned: the Empress Matilda, who fought Stephen for the throne; Edward V, who was put in the Tower by his uncle Richard III and didn't come out again; Edward VIII, who abdicated in 1936; and Edward VI's cousin Jane, who in 1554, at the age of 16, was proclaimed queen, deposed, arrested and executed in the space of just nine days.

Poor Jane had at least one qualification for the role of English monarch: a deep-seated aversion to hard work. She was, she said, 'ordained to touch crowns and sceptres, not needles and spindles'.

Henry VIII's daughter Elizabeth succeeded her half-sister Mary (England's first post-Norman queen) in 1558. Given the many glories of the Elizabethan Age that followed, it's easy to forget that science as we know it was still in its infancy – and that there were still some pretty funny ideas floating around. For example, both Sir Francis Drake (c.1540–1596) and Francis Bacon (1561–1626) believed in the principle of 'sympathetic magic', whereby, for example, a wound made by a dagger could be healed by dipping the dagger in the victim's blood (the philosopher John Locke believed in it too, even though he was born in 1632 and should have known better).

It was all very backward. You almost certainly wouldn't see any such nonsense being peddled by alternative-medicine quacks today. Almost certainly.

Sir Francis Drake, as we all know, was a famous ~~pirate~~ sea captain who in 1588 interrupted his game of bowls to see off

the Spanish Armada. It was a great moment in English history – and, indirectly, a great moment in English philosophy, too.

The esteemed philosopher Thomas Hobbes, author of *Leviathan*, was born in 1588 – because his mother, it was said 'fell in labour with him upon the fright of the Invasion of the Spaniards'.

Drake's buccaneering – what one biographer has called 'his unfortunate attraction to piracy' – wasn't as much of an embarrassment as it might have been, because in Elizabeth's England, piracy wasn't really piracy, as long as you were doing it to foreigners. English sea captains who had been robbed by foreign sailors could be issued by the authorities with a 'Letter of Reprisal'. This was a piece of paper that allowed them to recoup their losses by robbing other foreign sailors – any foreign sailors.

Drake's death in 1596 came at sea and during battle – but not quite in the all-guns-blazing manner one might expect. Yes, he was attacking Puerto Rico at the time. But his final action in battle came when a volley of fire from the shore blew him off his stool while he was eating his dinner. Drake, already ill, died soon afterwards.

Drake had made it abundantly clear that he wished to be buried on land. But the English have never paid much heed to such wishes where celebrities are concerned – so Drake's men bunged him in a lead-lined coffin, and buried him at sea.

Another of Elizabeth's splendid adventuring heroes/piratical bastards suffered a different kind of indignity. The illustrious Sir Walter Raleigh – explorer, free thinker, tobacco enthusiast – was nicknamed 'Water' Raleigh by the queen – because, being from the West Country, that was how he pronounced his own name.

The writer and broadcaster Stephen Fry once remarked: 'If our history of bear-baiting, pit ponies and ejected Christmas puppies can honestly be called a great British love affair with animals, then the average praying mantis and her husband are Darby and Joan.' He might have had a point. Animal-lovers, look away now.

Anti-Catholic feeling among England's Protestants grew to fever pitch during Elizabeth's reign. One way of expressing this sentiment was to construct huge wicker effigies of the Pope, and then burn them. What does this have to do with animals?

The effigies would often be stuffed with live cats before they were set alight – to give the impression that the Pope was screaming as he burned.

The anti-Catholic hysteria was heightened in 1598 when one Edward Squire, a supposed convert to the Church of Rome, was convicted of treason for plotting with the Spanish to assassinate Elizabeth. It was alleged – not hugely convincingly – that Squire had been hired by Spanish Jesuits to kill the queen by rubbing poison into the saddle of her horse. It was a rather ridiculous charge and Squire was probably innocent – but that didn't save him from being hanged, disembowelled and cut into pieces.

A ghastly death of a rather different kind came in 1594 to Ferdinando Stanley, 5th Earl of Derby – a nobleman who, until his father's death a year before his own, had the magnificent title Lord Strange, and would deserve a place in this book on that account alone. But there was more to Lord Strange than that.

He was, for one thing a major patron of the arts, sponsoring numerous poets and subsidising the acting company 'Strange's Men' – which included promising young actor W. Shakespeare.

On inheriting his father's title, Stanley was drawn away from the arts and into some deeply murky politics. A cabal of Catholic plotters, led by Richard Hesketh, approached Stanley with the proposal that he should lead a Spanish-backed revolt against Queen Elizabeth, and take the crown for himself – for Stanley was the great-grandson of Henry VIII's youngest

sister, and therefore had what might pass in bad light for a legitimate claim to the throne.

But Stanley turned down the offer, and loyally turned the plotters in (proving that he was – wait for it! – not only STRANGE but TRUE).

Then came his ghastly – and suspicious – death. The chronicler Stow provided a stomach-turning day-by-day account of his decline and demise, noting, among other things, that his vomit was 'verie grosse and fattie' (and its smell 'not without offence') and that his urine was 'in colour, smell and substance not unlike his vomites'.

Stanley died believing that he had been killed by witches.

Elizabeth died in 1603, at the age of 70 – impressive, especially given the brush with death she had experienced when she was 29. In October 1562, Elizabeth was struck down by the dreaded smallpox. As she hovered on the verge of death, England stumbled to the brink of constitutional crisis. The crisis passed – but the queen was left scarred and bald.

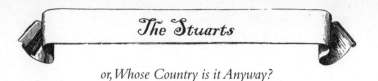

The Stuarts

or, Whose Country is it Anyway?

Puzzle time!

Here's a lateral-thinking puzzle for you. When Charles I was led to the chopping block on 30 January 1649, he was, by his own choice, wearing two shirts. Why? Answer at the end of the chapter …

Before we get on to Charles, we have to deal with his father, James I. He was a rewardingly strange king. If this book were called 'Scottish History: Strange but True', we'd be calling him James VI, but it isn't, so we're not. James, the son of Mary,

Queen of Scots, became king of both countries in 1603 – and ruler of the largest kingdom ruled by an English monarch since Oswy in the seventh century.

The English responded to James' accession to the throne with a tremendous show of joy. The festivities that greeted his arrival in London in the summer of 1603 almost overshadowed the outbreak of plague that hit the city at about the same time and left a quarter of the population dead.

James stopped off on his way from Scotland to London for a spot of browsing and sluicing at the home of one of his loyal supporters – Oliver Cromwell. No, this wasn't the Oliver Cromwell who, a generation later, would put James' son to death. This one had a knighthood, for one thing; he was the other Oliver's uncle.

We have James to thank for one of the most enduring symbols of his united kingdom: the Union Jack. The new king insisted that the flag be flown by all British ships (it's even been suggested that the flag's name comes from *Jacobus*, Latin for James). The flag, of course, caught on – but only after an almighty set-to between the heralds of England and Scotland over whose cross should be more prominent.

James really hated two things: tobacco, and witches.

He had, he was sure, encountered a number of witches during his time in Scotland and, although his enthusiasm for the cause came and went, in 1597 he wrote a book on the subject,

Daemonologie, which warned of 'the fearefull aboundinge at this time in this countrie of these detestable slaves of the Devil … witches'.

In 1604, now sitting comfortably on the English throne, James turned his attention to Walter Raleigh's detestable weed, tobacco. You couldn't accuse him of pussy-footing around the subject. Smoking tobacco, he wrote, was 'a custome lothsome to the eye, hatefull to the Nose, harmefull to the braine, dangerous to the Lungs, and in the blacke stinking fume thereof, neerest resembling the horrible Stigian smoke of the pit that is bottomelesse'. They should put that on the health warnings. He was still at it in 1619, when he condemned 'Tobacco-drunkardes'.

James' own health was sometimes a cause for curiosity, if not concern. In 1613, De Mayerne, James' court physician, pointed out that His Majesty's urine was often purple – the 'colour of Alicante wine'.

King James was also gay, or at least bisexual. Not that anyone at the time really gave a damn. 'Neither in Scotland nor in England,' biographer Jenny Wormald writes, 'were the king's sexual proclivities of as much interest in his day as they later became.'

No, what really annoyed James' enemies was the fact that he was – gasp! – a Scot. Among the most rabid of these anti-Scottish bigots were Robert Catesby, Ambrose Rookwood, Everard Digby[3], Guy Fawkes, and the other men remembered today as the Gunpowder Plotters. Of course, the ongoing oppression of Catholics throughout the kingdom also had something to do with the plotters' rebellion, but Scotophobia was certainly a factor; the plotters had privately voiced their desire to 'blow the Scots back to Scotland'. Guy Fawkes – who changed his name to 'Guido' to show his support for Catholic Spain – wrote of 'the natural hostility between English and Scots' in his correspondence with the Spanish authorities.

Fawkes wasn't the leader of the plot (that was Catesby), but he arguably paid the highest price for his insurrection. While Catesby was shot in action, Fawkes was captured, and subjected to torture so brutal that he was barely able to sign his name on his confession (see below). He was then hanged, drawn and quartered.

We're still (kind of) following the order put out by the authorities in 1606, the year after the plot, for events of 'Public Thanksgiving to Almighty God every year on the fifth Day of November'. For a long time, Guy Fawkes Night was a welcome excuse for Protestants to bash Catholics; now, of course, it's mostly about fireworks and jacket potatoes.

Few monarchs have written as much – or as well – as James I. And he could write poetry as well as polemics. His last poem – an answer to those in England who 'libelled' him, although we don't know the details of the libel in question – asked:

> You that knowe me all soe well
> Why do you push me down to hell
> By making me an Infidell?

Two years later James was dead.

As we have seen in the sorry case of Henry VI, a kingship can't quite be described as a roaring success if it concludes with the king in prison and the nation in a state of civil war. If it comes to an end with the king having his head chopped off, it's definitely been a below par bit of reigning.

Thus it was for Charles I, under whose reign all hell broke loose.

Charles was very taken with the idea of the Divine Right of Kings – the principle that the king was God's anointed and therefore answerable only to the Almighty. You can see why the idea would appeal to kings generally.

But it wasn't the only odd idea Charles held dear. The idea that the touch of a king could cure scrofula – a ghastly disease now known as mycobacterial cervical lymphadenitis, but then known as 'the king's evil' – dated from the Middle Ages, and the custom was enshrined in the *Book of Common Prayer* in 1633, nine years into Charles' rule.

In 1712, the infant Samuel Johnson – later famous as a dictionary-drudge and all-round wiseacre – was 'touched' for the scrofula by Queen Anne. King Charles II was said to have placed his healing hands on a total of 92,000 ailing persons (and, knowing him, on a similar number of non-ailing persons). On one occasion, six people hoping to be healed by Charles II ended up being trampled to death in the crush.

The practice was discontinued in the eighteenth century by the Protestant George I, who considered it a bit Popish for his tastes, but it had been a subject of mockery long before then. In the irreverent 1640s, radical journalists made merciless fun of a story claiming that a sick child had been restored to health thanks to the holy properties of the spittle of Charles I.

Most cruelly of all, the roughneck Parliamentarians who guarded Charles after his capture in 1647 also made mock of the king's belief in 'touching'. They nicknamed him 'Stroker'.

All that was yet to come, of course, when Charles took the throne in 1625. He was a vigorous man and an impressive speaker – despite suffering since childhood from weak ankles (caused by rickets) and a pronounced stutter.

One of the most curious characters at Charles' court was a young man named Jeffery Hudson. His introduction to the king and queen, when he was just 8 years old, had been spectacular: Jeffery, who then stood 18in tall, sprang out of a huge pie baked in the royal couple's honour.

He eventually grew to around 3ft 9in in the course of a life filled with adventure. He turned up in 1640, at the 'bedding ceremony' of William II, Prince of Orange's new bride Princess Mary: Jeffery's role was to produce a large pair of shears with which to cut the stitches of the bride's nightdress. When, returning from a voyage to France, he was kidnapped by pirates, it was reported that the court was more upset 'than if it had lost an entire fleet'. In 1644, Hudson challenged a gentleman named Crofts to a duel. Crofts turned up armed only with a giant water-squirt, with which he teased the angry dwarf; Hudson had turned up with a gun, with which he shot Crofts through the head.

Hudson was painted for posterity alongside the 7ft 6in William Evans. Also muscling in on the portrait was a man named Thomas Parr, who claimed to be 152 years old but wasn't.

Beyond the finery of the court, Charles' England was becoming an increasingly unsettled place, a land of growing dissent and murmured heresies. But if these heresies became loud enough for the Church to hear, the Church cracked down hard.

In 1637, for example, the physician John Bastwick, the barrister William Prynne and the minister Robert Burton all had their ears hacked off for daring to criticise the bishops of the established Church. In 1641, Richard Overton wrote a play entitled *Canterbury, his Change of Diet*, in which the Archbishop of Canterbury – the hated William Laud – insisted on feasting on 'the tippets' of men's ears.

The Levellers were among the many Nonconformist political and religious sects that emerged in the turbulent 1640s (others included the Diggers, the Ranters and the less-catchily titled Grindletonians). The Levellers were in favour, fundamentally, of reforming the whole establishment of England, transforming its church and political constitution, and restoring civil rights to the common man. These ideas were, of course, pretty radical at the time – but not to the Levellers, who called their newspaper *The Moderate*.

Another group of Nonconformists made a lasting imprint on English politics at this time – but not in the way they might have hoped.

The Scottish Presbyterian 'Covenanters' who marched on Edinburgh in rebellion against Charles' reign in 1648 were seen by some as representing the lowest classes of Scottish society – the kind of people who regarded sour milk, or whigg, as a staple foodstuff (and many did). The Covenanters' march to the capital became known by satirists as 'the March of the Whiggamores' or 'sour-milk men'. Whiggamore soon became Whig, and its meaning was expanded to include not just Covenanters but anyone who defended the Protestant succession. The term became central to the English political vocabulary. Robert Walpole, Charles James Fox, Edmund Burke, Thomas Macaulay – all sour-milk men, and proud of it. (The opposing political term also stems from this period, and is also not English in origin: 'Tory' comes from *tóraidhe*, a Gaelic word for a dispossessed Irish outlaw.)

Savage as religious persecution could be in the mid-1600s, there were ways of dodging punishment. The Ranter Abiezer Coppe, for instance, was examined by a parliamentary committee in 1650. Presumably keen on keeping hold of his ear-tippets, Coppe took the prudent step of pretending to be insane, 'flinging apples and pears about the room'. Quite why apples and pears were provided by the parliamentary committee is a different question altogether.

It's important to remember that these were still deeply brutal times, and England was a deeply brutal country. It was by no means alone in this, of course – but the English were certainly capable of appalling their Continental neighbours. In the mid-1600s, for example, Dutch merchants were horrified by the Englishman's habit of beating his wife (though the practice was generally frowned on in Yorkshire).

And yet, England in the seventeenth century produced many men and women of exceptional genius.

The poet John Milton was one such. You could tell he was a smart one, a contemporary noted, because he rolled his Rs when he spoke – 'a certaine signe of a Satyricall wit'. Milton was known at Oxford as 'the Lady of Christ's College' because of his exceedingly fair skin.

Then there was Isaac Newton. Much as Alfred the Great was a good king but a rubbish baker, Newton was a good scientist but a pretty shoddy shepherd: asked to tend to the sheep on his mother's farm as a young man, he instead passed the time building models of waterwheels – while the sheep went marauding through the neighbours' fields. Newton probably wouldn't have seen the funny side. Humphrey Newton, his assistant at Cambridge for five years, said that in all that time he saw the great scientist laugh only once – when someone asked him what the point was in studying Euclid.

The Civil War began in (riffles through textbook, comes up empty-handed, sighs, starts again …)

At least one eminent historian has noted that 'it is difficult to say exactly when and where the Civil War broke out'. But we can have a go at explaining why it broke out. Much of it was to do with Charles' authoritarian rule, unfair taxation and the rise of Nonconformism. But at least a tiny part of it concerned not power or money or religion – but sex. Sort of.

Robert Devereux, Earl of Essex, was one of the Parliamentarians' leading lights in the early 1640s. A career soldier, he became the supreme commander of the Parliamentary land forces in June 1641; at the first proper set-to of the war, at Edgehill, he led the 'Roundheads' against Charles' men. Devereux's opposition to the king may have had its roots in political conviction. But he had a personal axe to grind, too. As a young man, he had been fearfully humiliated when James I, Charles' father, connived in having his marriage to Frances Howard annulled – on grounds of sexual impotence.

It's the sort of thing that could make a man bear a grudge.

Parliament's split with the king was pretty much irremediable by autumn 1640. Such was the authority of the Commons that the firebrand MP John Pym, whose signature adorned many of parliament's 'ordinances', became known as 'King Pym'.

The bit of English history that comes after Charles I and before Charles II is known as the Interregnum. This means 'between reigns', so obviously people at the time didn't call it that. They didn't know that there another king was on the way (in fact, many people thought it more probable that the Second Coming of Christ was on the way).

So they called it the Protectorate, and they called Oliver Cromwell the Lord Protector. After a while, they even asked him to be king, but he wasn't the sort to stand for such nonsense; he was a man of simple needs, and, as long as he was allowed absolute, unquestioned power over the entire country, he had no wish for such baubles as crowns and sceptres.

It was a peaceful, harmonious time. During Cromwell's Protectorate, the government needed just 6,000 soldiers to maintain order in England. (This being a book about England, the fact that keeping the peace in Scotland and Ireland required more than 40,000 soldiers is beyond our jurisdiction.)

Cromwell was, of course, a sternly religious man. But even he was taken aback by the treatment meted out – after weeks of furious debate in parliament and the courts – to the Quaker James Nayler in 1656. 'Sternly religious' barely begins to describe it.

In October '56, Nayler rode into Bristol while his Quaker companions cast garments before him and sang 'Holy, Holy, Holy, Lord God of Sabbath' – an (at the time) unmistakeable imitation of Christ's entry into Jerusalem on Palm Sunday. This was, perhaps, unwise.

At trial, Nayler was found guilty of impersonating Christ and of claiming divine status. He was sentenced to be whipped through the streets by the hangman, clapped in the pillory, have his tongue bored through with a red-hot iron, and have the letter 'B' for blasphemy branded on his forehead. He was then to be returned to Bristol and forced to ride out of the city sitting backwards on his horse (probably a welcome bit of light relief after the tongue-boring and head-branding). Finally, he was to be committed to solitary confinement in Bridewell.

Nayler didn't endure these torments alone, though; his supporters joined him in the pillory. One of them, the merchant Robert Rich, put up a notice that read 'This is the King of the Jews' – and licked Nayler's wounds.

Others did rather better out of the Protectorate. Thomas Pride, the Puritan soldier who signed Charles I's death warrant and in 1648 supervised a notorious purge of conservative MPs, capitalised on his associations with the Protectorate to land a lucrative contract for supplying beer to the Royal Navy. It was not, however, very good beer. On one occasion, Pride admitted, the navy had deemed a £1,600 delivery of his beer to be unfit for consumption – and had tossed it overboard.

After Richard 'Tumbledown Dick' Cromwell was forced to resign from the Commonwealth of England in 1659, the governance of the country went somewhat to ruin. The army was divided; Parliament was a shambles. By the time General Monck marched down to London and started cracking heads together in February 1660, public opinion of the Commons and Lords had sunk so low that, according to Pepys, 'boys do now cry "Kiss my Parliament!" instead of "Kiss my arse!"'

After the Restoration, in 1661, it was decided that it was high time Oliver Cromwell was punished for being so beastly to the old king, and that he oughtn't be allowed to weasel out of it on a technicality – viz, having been dead since 1658.

FAC-SIMILE OF THE WARRANT FOR THE EXECUTION OF CHARLES I.

A.D. 1648.

Cromwell's body, along with those of the regicides Henry Ireton and John Bradshaw, was dug up in January 1661. It was hanged, beheaded, and dumped in an unmarked grave beneath the Tyburn gallows.

Another regicide, Thomas Harrison, was unfortunate enough to live long enough to witness his own execution. Harrison's hands and knees were seen to tremble on the scaffold, but Harrison said that that was 'by reason of much blood I have lost in the wars, and many wounds I have received in my body'. According to one source, the sentence of hanging, drawing and quartering 'was so barbarously executed, that he was cut down alive, and saw his bowels thrown into the fire'.

Another account offers a more action-packed version, with the unrepentant Harrison struggling to his feet (while being quartered) and boxing his executioner about the ears.

The Civil War had come to a weary, blood-soaked end at Worcester in 1651. Cromwell had destroyed what remained of the Royalist army – by this time mostly Scotsmen recruited by Charles' son, Charles.

The younger Charles' escape in the wake of the Battle of Worcester was a classic episode of cavalier derring-do. Sneaking incognito across England en route to asylum in France, Charles was required variously to hide up a tree (the famous 'Boscobel Oak'), cut off his hair, pose as a servant, shoe horses, and, finally, be carried ashore in France on the shoulders of his ship's mate. His return to England in May 1660 was rather more glamorous. But it wasn't all fine words, grand robes and fancy hairpieces – as sharp-eyed Samuel Pepys pointed out.

As the king was rowed ashore from his ship *The Royal Charles* (formerly the *Naseby*), Pepys followed behind in another boat, along with 'a dog that the King loved (which did sh*t in the boat), which made us laugh and me think that a King and all that belong to him are but just as others are'.

Charles II was declared king in May, 1660. Charles himself, however, dated the beginning of his reign back to 1649 and the execution of his father (effectively wiping Cromwell's Protectorate from the history books). His reign of twenty-five years, then, should be considered a reign of forty-four years – a reign as long as that of Elizabeth I.

One of the most remarkable things about the Restoration of the Monarchy was the apparent ease with which the army – which had, in effect, been running the country for some time – was put back in its box. It quite simply melted away, as recorded in Pepys' Diary of 1663: 'This Captain turned a shoemaker; the lieutenant, a baker; this, a brewer; that a haberdasher; this common soldier, a porter; and every man in his apron and frock, &c, as if they had never done anything else.' The minister Richard Baxter observed: 'Thus did God do a more wonderful work in the dissolving of this army than any of their greatest victories.'

The Restoration famously saw London's theatres reopen after years of Puritan austerity. Most shockingly, the theatre managers – and the censors – now allowed women on stage. Women! Playing women! An outrage.

The first words ever spoken by a woman on the public stage in London were 'My noble father, I do perceive here a divided duty' – not the most powerful statement of liberation, but certainly a start. They're the first words spoken by Desdemona in *Othello*.

Scandalous talk and outrageous repartee wasn't restricted to the theatres in Restoration London; it ran wild in the city's coffee-houses, too. Charles II, so indulgent of his beloved playhouses (and beloved actresses),[4] was less enamoured of these newfangled proto-Starbucks. They were, he wrote, 'places where the boldest Calumnies and Scandals were raised, and discoursed among a people who know not each other'.

He was fighting against the tide. By 1739, there were 551 coffee houses in London alone – roughly one for every 1,000 people.

Of course, with all this new social life around the place, fashion came on in leaps and bounds. Feathered hats and ribboned shoes were *de rigeur* for gentlemen. The French fashion for wigs – or 'counterfeit hair' as one disapproving commentator called them – spread like wildfire. Trouser-legs grew to preposterous widths: Pepys wrote of a man 'who put both his legs through one of his Knees of his breeches, and went so all day'.

At Charles' coronation, the ludicrously swashbuckling Duke of Buckingham went all-out in the fashion stakes. His jewel-encrusted suit was rumoured to have cost him £10,000. (Buckingham wasn't always so fussy about his dress: after killing the husband of his mistress Anna Maria Talbot in the most notorious duel of the age in 1688, he made love to her – while still wearing his bloodstained shirt).

But the good times couldn't last. Soon London found itself once again under the hammer. Yes, War had gone – but that left the field free for Pestilence to strut its stuff. Bubonic plague was spread by fleas that were carried by rats that were pretty much everywhere in the dirty old town that was London in the seventeenth century. We all know that now – but nobody at all knew it then. Except, perhaps, one man.

Remember Theodore de Mayerne, the observant medic who noted that James I's urine was rather more wine-coloured than is usual? In 1630, that same de Mayerne had called for the introduction of forty-day plague quarantines and the creation of a London board of health to combat the dreaded pestilence – and suggested that the plague might be carried from person to person by 'rats, mice, weasels and such vermin'.

There's something presumptuous about calling the outbreak of bubo-ridden death that seized London in 1665 'the plague'. It was a plague, yes – but was it really all that different from, say, that of 1499–1500 (in which it was said, implausibly, that 20,000 Londoners died)? Or that of 1511? Or 1563? Or 1578, 1582, 1593, 1603, 1609, 1625 or 1636?

The so-called 'Great Plague' of 1665 was a humdinger, though: total deaths in London that year were in excess of 97,000, more than five times the usual number and perhaps 20 per cent of the city's population. But the plagues of 1603 and 1625 took just as great a toll, relative to population, and that of 1563 resulted in a body count eight times the usual yearly figure.

So there was nothing particularly great about the Great Plague. In all probability, the plague of summer 1665 is remembered mainly because it was followed, in summer 1666, by …

… the Great Fire of London, of course, which was great in some ways but not really in others.

As William Fitzstephen observed in the 1170s, fires were a day-to-day hazard for the medieval Londoner. Fitzstephen would have known of the major blazes in 1077, 1087, 1092, 1133 and 1136. But the Great Fire really was the big one; after this, London would never be the same again.

A generall Bill for this present year,

ending the 19 of *December* 1665. according to the Report made to the KINGS most Excellent Majesty.

By the Company of Parish Clerks of *London*, &c.

	Buried	Plag.		Buried	Plag.		Buried	Plag.		Buried	Plag.
St Albans Woodstreet	200	121	St Clements Eastcheap	38	20	St Margaret Moses	38	25	St Michael Cornhill	104	52
St Alhallowes Barking	514	330	St Dionis Backchurch	78	27	St Margaret Newfishstreet	114	66	St Michael Crookedlane	179	133
St Alhallowes Breadstreet	35	16	St Dunstans East	265	150	St Margaret Pattons	49	24	St Michael Queenhithe	203	122
St Alhallowes Great	455	426	St Edmunds Lombardstreet	70	36	St Mary Abchurch	99	54	St Michael Quern	44	18
St Alhallowes Honilane	10	5	St Ethelborough	195	106	St Mary Aldermanbury	181	109	St Michael Royall	152	116
St Alhallowes Lesse	239	175	St Faiths	104	70	St Mary Aldermary	105	75	St Michael Woodstreet	122	62
St Alhall. Lombardstreet	90	62	St Fosters	144	105	St Mary le Bow	64	36	St Mildred Breadstreet	59	26
St Alhallowes Staining	185	112	St Gabriel Fen church	69	39	St Mary Bothaw	55	30	St Mildred Poultrey	68	46
St Alhallowes the Wall	500	356	St George Botolphlane	41	27	St Mary Colechurch	17	6	St Nicholas Acons	46	28
St Alphage	271	115	St Gregories by Pauls	376	232	St Mary Hill	94	64	St Nicholas Coleabby	125	91
St Andrew Hubbard	71	25	St Hellens	108	75	St Mary Mounthaw	56	37	St Nicholas Olaves	90	62
St Andrew Undershaft	274	189	St James Dukes place	262	190	St Mary Summerset	342	262	St Olaves Hartstreet	237	160
St Andrew Wardrobe	476	308	St James Garlickhithe	189	118	St Mary Stayning	47	27	St Olaves Jewry	54	32
St Anne Aldersgate	282	197	St John Baptist	138	83	St Mary Woolchurch	65	33	St Olaves Silverstreete	250	132
St Anne Blacke-Friers	652	467	St John Evangelist	9		St Mary Woolnoth	75	38	St Pancras Soperlane	30	15
St Antholins Parish	58	33	St John Zacharie	85	54	St Martins Iremongerlane	21	11	St Peters Cheape	61	35
St Austins Parish	43	20	St Katherine Coleman	299	213	St Martins Ludgate	196	128	St Peters Cornehill	136	76
St Barthol. Exchange	73	51	St Katherine Creechurch	335	231	St Martins Orgars	110	71	St Peters Pauls Wharfe	114	86
St Bennet Fynch	47	22	St Lawrence Jewry	94	48	St Martins Outwich	60	34	St Peters Poore	79	47
St Benn. Gracechurch	57	41	St Lawrence Pountney	214	140	St Martins Vintrey	417	349	St Stevens Colmanstreet	560	391
St Bennet Pauls Wharf	355	172	St Leonard Eastcheap	42	27	St Matthew Fridaystreet	24	6	St Stevens Walbrooke	34	17
St Bennet Sherehog	11	1	St Leonard Fosterlane	335	255	St Maudlins Milkstreet	44	22	St Swithins	93	56
St Botolph Billingsgate	83	50	St Magnus Parish	103	60	St Maudlins Oldfishstreet	176	121	St Thomas Apostle	163	110
Christs Church	653	467	St Margaret Lothbury	100	66	St Michael Bassishaw	253	164	Trinitie Parish	115	79
St Christophers	60	47									

Buried in the 97 Parishes within the walls, — 15207 *Whereof, of the Plague* — 9887

	Buried	Plag.		Buried	Plag.		Buried	Plag.		Buried	Plag.
St Andrew Holborne	3958	3103	Bridewell Precinct	230	179	St Dunstans West	958	665	St Saviours Southwark	4235	3446
St Bartholmew Great	493	344	St Botolph Aldersgate	997	755	St George Southwark	1613	1260	St Sepulchres Parish	4509	2746
St Bartholmew Lesse	193	139	St Botolph Algate	4926	4051	St Giles Cripplegate	8069	4838	St Thomas Southwark	475	371
St Bridget	2111	1427	St Botolph Bishopsgate	3464	2500	St Olaves Southwark	4793	2785	Trinity Minories	168	123
									At the Pesthouse	159	156

Buried in the 16 Parishes without the walls — 41351 *Whereof, of the Plague* — 28888

	Buried	Plag.		Buried	Plag.		Buried	Plag.		Buried	Plag.
St Giles in the Fields	4457	3216	St Katherines Tower	956	601	St Magdalen Bermondsey	1943	1363	St Mary Whitechappel	4766	3855
Hackney Parish	232	132	Lambeth Parish	798	537	St Mary Newington	1272	1004	Redriffe Parish	304	210
St James Clarkenwel	1863	1377	St Leonard Shoreditch	2669	1949	St Mary Islington	696	593	Stepney Parish	8598	6583

Buried in the 12 out-Parishes, in Middlesex and Surrey — 28554 *Whereof, of the Plague* — 21420

	Buried	Plag.		Buried	Plag.
St Clement Danes	1969	1319	St Mary Savoy	303	198
St Paul Covent Garden	408	261	St Margaret Westminst.	4710	3742
St Martins in the Fields	4804	2883	whereof at the Pesthouse		156

Buried in the 5 Parishes in the City and Liberties of Westminster — 12194
whereof, of the Plague — 8403

The Total of all the Christnings — 9967
The Total of all the Burials this year — 97306
Whereof, of the Plague — 68596

The Diseases and Casualties this year.

Abortive and Stilborne	617	Executed	21	Palsie	30
Aged	1545	Flox and Small Pox	655	Plague	68596
Ague and Feaver	5257	Found dead in streets, fields, &c.	20	Plannet	6
Appoplex and Suddenly	116	French Pox	86	Plurisie	15
Bedrid	10	Frighted	23	Poysoned	1
Blasted	5	Gout and Sciatica	27	Quinsie	35
Bleeding	16	Grief	46	Rickets	557
Bloody Flux, Scowring & Flux	185	Griping in the Guts	1288	Rising of the Lights	397
Burnt and Scalded	8	Hangd & made away themselves	7	Rupture	34
Calenture	3	Headmouldshot & Mouldfallen	14	Scurvy	105
Cancer, Gangrene and Fistula	56	Jaundies	110	Shingles and Swine pox	2
Canker, and Thrush	111	Impostume	227	Sores, Ulcers, broken and bruised Limbs	82
Childbed	625	Kild by severall accidents	46	Spleen	14
Chrisomes and Infants	1258	Kings Evill	86	Spotted Feaver and Purples	1929
Cold and Cough	68	Leprosie	2	Stopping of the stomack	332
Collick and Winde	134	Lethargy	14	Stone and Strangury	98
Consumption and Tissick	4808	Livergrown	20	Surfet	1251
Convulsion and Mother	2036	Meagrom and Headach	12	Teeth and Worms	2614
Distracted	5	Measles	7	Vomiting	51
Dropsie and Timpany	1478	Murthered and Shot	9	Wenn	1
Drowned	50	Overlaid & Starved	45		

Christned { Males — 5114; Females — 4853; In all — 9967 }

Buried { Males — 48569; Females — 48737; In all — 97306 } Of the Plague — 68596

Increased in the Burials in the 130 Parishes and at the Pest-house this year — 79009

Increased of the Plague in the 130 Parishes and at the Pest-house this year — 68590

As everyone knows, the Great Fire of London started in a neglected bread oven in a bakery on Pudding Lane.

Or did it?

Well, yes, it probably did, but that didn't stop the conspiracy theorists. In 1681, an inscription was placed in Pudding Lane to mark the place where 'Hell broke loose upon this Protestant City from the malicious hearts of barbarous Papists, by ye hand of their Agent Hubert'.[5] Who?

Robert Hubert was a young Frenchman who, in September 1666, confessed to starting the fire in Thomas Farriner's Pudding Lane bakery. His 'confession' was muddled, unconvincing and unsupported by the evidence – even the government thought him deranged. But that didn't stop the conspiracy theorists. Hubert was hanged at Tyburn; it was reported that, afterwards, the enraged crowd tore his body to pieces.

The public anger directed at Hubert shows just how much hatred there was in England for Catholics. As it happened, Hubert was a Protestant, not a Catholic – but that didn't stop the conspiracy theorists. Nothing ever does.

Incidentally, Hubert's conviction meant that the fire was technically an act of war (since Hubert was French, and England was at war with France). This neat bit of legal finesse meant that the obligation to rebuild the ruined city did not lie, as it would otherwise have done, with the unfortunate tenants of the damaged buildings – and, in effect, made possible the city's reconstruction.

As the wildfire spread through the city like, well, wildfire, Londoners – seeing that there was little chance of dampening down the blaze – hurried to secure their possessions. Samuel Pepys, for instance, buried his private papers to keep them

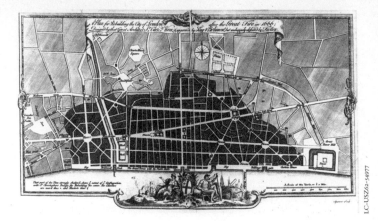

safe from the flames – along with his wine collection and a Parmesan cheese. It wasn't just humans who suffered in the Great Fire. London's pigeons had a hard time of it too. 'The poor pigeons,' Pepys observed, 'were loth to leave their houses, but hovered about the windows and balconys till they were, some of them burned, their wings, and fell down.'

Despite the devastation, only nine people were known to have died in the fire. The total value of property destroyed, however, was estimated at £10 million; the fire consumed eighty-seven parish churches, forty-four Company halls, and some 13,200 houses. (The extent of the damage is shown above.) The cheerful verdict of Lord Mayor Sir Thomas Bludworth when the fire first took hold – 'A woman could piss it out!' – could hardly have been more wrong.

Charles II died in February 1685. James II, Charles' younger brother, was a pretty poor king, but, on the plus side, at least he wasn't around for long. His reign of three-and-a-bit years might have been even shorter – there was no shortage of rebels ready to kick him off the throne.

Most significant was the Monmouth Rebellion of 1685. Like the rising of the 1640s, it began with anti-royal anger and ended with someone getting his head chopped off. But that someone wasn't the king.

James Scott, the Duke of Monmouth, was the illegitimate son of Charles II and his mistress Lucy Walter – 'the first of Charles II's many bastards', as one historian has put it. He grew up to be an ill-educated and violent gadabout, but he was a Protestant ill-educated violent gadabout, and that was what mattered. A rumour therefore sprang up that Charles and Lucy had been married in secret back in the 1640s – and that therefore Monmouth had a serious claim to the throne. To make it all that bit more exciting, there was talk of a mysterious 'black box' that contained the marriage documents.

You will be amazed to learn that no such 'black box' was ever found.

Soon Monmouth was the toast of England's Protestant Whigs, and streets ahead of his uncle James in the popularity stakes. But you don't get to be king just because people like you – what do you think this is, a democracy?

So Monmouth launched his rebellion, landing (like the Black Death) in Dorset and (like the Black Death) swiftly overwhelming the south-west. In the end, however, he proved rather easier to get shot of than the Black Death: his rebel army was routed at Sedgeworth, and Monmouth himself was found hiding in a ditch, taken to London, and sentenced to death.

His execution was pure theatre – if you like your theatre bloody.

The (Whiggish) historian Macaulay reported that, upon the scaffold, Monmouth – 'the darling of the people' – said little. 'I come here,' he told the crowd, 'not to speak, but to die.' He then approached his executioner, Jack Ketch, and said: 'Here are six guineas for you. Do not hack me as you did my Lord Russell.' (Russell, Monmouth's co-conspirator, had been clumsily beheaded in July 1683.)

Monmouth thumbed the executioner's axe, and voiced doubts about its sharpness. Then he knelt to the block. Ketch, 6 guineas notwithstanding, muffed the job. The first blow only wounded Monmouth; the Duke 'struggled, rose from the block, and looked reproachfully at the executioner'.

Ketch swung the axe again, and again — but still the head wasn't severed, and still Monmouth struggled on the block.

According to Macaulay, Ketch at this point threw down his axe and cried 'My heart fails me!' But eventually he was persuaded to finish what he had begun: two more blows, and Monmouth — like his royal grandfather before him — lay dead on the chopping block.

The crowd surged forward with two objectives: one, to dip their handkerchiefs in the blood of Monmouth, the Protestant martyr, and, two, to tear to shreds Jack Ketch, the cack-handed executioner, who was bundled to safety under heavy guard.

Shortly after the gruesome beheading of Russell, a document had appeared purporting to be written by Ketch himself, and entitled *The Apologie of John Ketch, Esq.* In it, Ketch indignantly denied the 'untrue Reports' regarding the execution — viz, that he had not turned up drunk, had not been paid 20 guineas the night before to do a neat job, had not struck Russell's shoulder with his first blow, and had not been thrown into Newgate prison for his incompetence. Instead, he blamed Russell for 'flinching' as the axe fell.

Unsurprisingly, Russell's and Monmouth's were the only beheadings (as opposed to hangings) that Ketch ever carried out. His name soon became a byname for the executioner of London. He reappeared in the early 1800s as a lead character in the first 'Punch & Judy' puppet shows — back when Punch & Judy was strictly an adult entertainment, fit more for a pub's back room than a seaside booth. In these shows, the murderous Punch would typically butcher his wife, the policeman, and Lucifer himself — before tricking Ketch into putting his head into his own noose.

James II was deposed and exiled in 1688. His son, James Francis, kept alive a Jacobite flame as 'the Old Pretender', the Stuart claimant to the throne – though many in England believed not only that the Stuarts had no right to the throne, but that James Francis wasn't even a real Stuart.

JAMES·II

Drawn by J.L.Williams

Engraved by Thos.Brown.

His birth in 1688 had been the subject of fierce controversy. English Protestants quite frankly could not abide the prospect of a Catholic heir to James II – and so, when it was announced that James' wife, Maria Beatrice d'Este of Modena, was pregnant, the Protestant community put on an impressive show of maintaining that black was white. Protestants invited to attend at the baby's birth pointedly turned their backs so as to avoid having to bear witness. Rumours circulated that another baby had been smuggled into the royal residence in a warming pan. A compilation of more than seventy eyewitness accounts of young James' birth was dismissed as untrustworthy.

This was a masterclass in wishful thinking. But the baby's Stuartness became a moot point in any case when, in November 1688, along came the Glorious Revolution, and England got two monarchs for the price of one.

Never mind the Anglo-Dutch Wars of 1652–54 (and 1665–67 and 1672–74) – on this occasion, religious bigotry trumped nationalistic jingoism and England invited the Protestant Dutchman, William, Prince of Orange, and his wife Mary, to take the throne.

The novelist Tobias Smollett said that William 'might have passed for one of the best princes of the age in which he lived, had he never ascended the throne of Great Britain'. Smollett went on to provide a handy summary of England's first Dutch monarch. He was, Smollett wrote, 'indefatigable in war, enterprising in politics, dead to all the warm and generous emotions of the human heart, a cold relation, an indifferent husband, a disagreeable man, an ungracious prince, and an imperious sovereign'.

You'd have to call that a mixed review.

Early in William III's reign, the ghost of the Sumptuary Laws was briefly resurrected as Parliament once again took it upon itself to instruct the people of England in what they really ought to be wearing this season. This time, though, the intent was not to preserve the exclusivity of pointy shoes but to save an industry: the Bill put before the House in 1789 enjoined subjects 'to wear the woollen manufacture at certain seasons of the year' in order to shore up the struggling textiles trade. The Bill was defeated following protests and rioting among the silk weavers of London and Canterbury, and so endured the Englishman's God-given right not to wear a woolly jumper unless he wants to.

The Battle of the Boyne of 1690 belongs to Irish history as much as to English history – but then, it has a pretty prominent place in the history of all of Europe, as the armies that clashed on the Boyne, one under William III and the other under the deposed James II, were a thoroughly cosmopolitan bunch. London-born James' Jacobites were French and Irish while Dutchman William led an Anglo-French-Dutch-Danish-Scottish-Irish force (with the help of a German-born general). It was all, in a sense, terribly British.

Little Englanders who object to the above remark might take comfort in reflecting that it's a lot easier to be a

Little Englander these days than it used to be. This is because England has got Littler. We are, for instance, almost a whole town lighter.

St Martin's was the first to go. St Leonard's followed soon after. St Nicholas put up a good fight but went next. Then it was John the Baptist. These were the churches of Dunwich; it was a good-sized town in the Middle Ages, and now there isn't any of it left at all. Or rather, there is a little bit, but most of it is somewhere at the bottom of the North Sea.

Like most places on England's east coast, Dunwich was at the mercy of the waves, which ate away at it day by day – and the churches crumbled one after another. By 1698, only one – All Saints – still stood, which meant that, in a psephological quirk, the small town now had more MPs than it did churches (thanks to dodgy electoral practices, the few remaining Dunwichians were allowed to elect two).

A few hundred years later, in 1919, All Saints finally took the plunge too. The church and half of the graveyard fell into the ocean – leaving the bones of the corpses buried in the graveyard sticking horridly out of the cliff face.

Queen Anne, who succeeded brother-in-law William III in 1702, was the second daughter of James II. Six of her brothers and sisters had died in infancy – a sad foreshadowing of what was to come. Anne conceived eighteen children. None survived her.

Anne was the last Stuart monarch. The Stuart line, however, persists to this day. Should England ever decide that the Jacobites were right after all and what we really need is a

Stuart on the throne, the man to call is Franz, the elderly Duke of Bavaria – Charles I's great-great-great-great-great-great-great-great-great-grandson.

As for King Charles' two shirts: 30 January 1649 was a cold day. Charles wore two shirts for warmth – not for his own comfort, but so that it could never be said that the King of England trembled in the face of death.

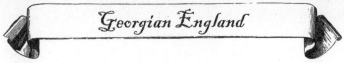
or, the Hanover Cure

Enter the Germans. The elector of Hanover, Georg Ludwig, dropped his 'Ludwig' and acquired an 'e' on his accession to the English throne in 1714. At 54, he was at the time the oldest person ever to take the throne.

He was King of Great Britain and Ireland before he'd even been there – he was proclaimed king on August 1, but didn't arrive in his new kingdom till 18 September. For the best part of two months, George I was 'the king over the water' (but you must never say so to a Jacobite, or they'll think you mean 'the Old Pretender', or James Francis Stuart, James II's son).

Not everyone was pleased by the arrival of the new king. Many Catholics considered him a usurper of the throne that belonged rightfully to James Francis Stuart. Others went further: they blamed George not only for butting in on the succession but for importing vermin.

An enduring legend among English Catholics maintained that the ship that brought George I to England also brought with it a cargo of brown rats – pestilential vermin previously unknown in this country (the English always having made do perfectly well with good old-fashioned home-grown black rats). The fact that this was nonsense didn't stop it persisting stubbornly well into the next century; the famous nineteenth-century naturalist Charles Waterton, best-known for creative taxidermy (including making a human face out of a monkey's bottom), insisted on calling the animal the 'Hanoverian Rat'.

George remained very Hanoverian and not very English throughout his reign. Unlike, say, William III, he never learned to speak much English. It was considered rude, however, to point this out. In 1717, the MP William Shippen noted that the king was 'unacquainted with our language and our constitution' – and was clapped in the Tower for his insolence.

George did make some effort with the language, though: he paid for English lessons for two of his German servants, so that they could read the English newspapers for him.

The Battle of Dettingen in June 1743 marked the last time (so far!) an English king led his troops into battle. By 'English king' we of course mean 'King of England', because George II, like his father, was born in Hanover (he maintained that he did not have a drop of blood that was not English, but, as he said it in a thick German accent, he wasn't fooling anybody). And the force he led against the French at Dettingen was appropriately multinational, comprising British, Hanoverian, Dutch and Hessian troops. The force was known, with typical Germanic whimsy, as 'The Pragmatic Army'.

At home, George was something of a grouch. On one occasion, the peer Lord Hervey reported, he 'snubbed the princess Emily for not hearing him, the princess Caroline for being grown fat, the Duke for standing awkwardly, [and] Lord Hervey for not knowing what relation the Prince of Sultzbach was to the Elector Palatine'. But then, look at what he had to put up with. At one point, according to Robert Walpole, Lady Deloraine was in disgrace for pulling the king's chair from under him. That's enough to put anyone in a bad mood.

George II also ticked off his queen, Caroline of Brandenburg-Ansbach, for behaving more like a schoolmistress than a wife, and dismissed her interest in books and writers as 'lettered nonsense'. He was not the only one to be less than besotted with Caroline. She was despised by the public, who regarded her (not entirely inaccurately) as the controlling power behind the throne. This gave rise to satirical rhymes such as:

You may strut, dapper George, but 'twill all be in vain;
We know 'tis Queen Caroline, not you, that reign.

Caroline's eldest son Frederick also fell out with her bitterly – and the antipathy was mutual. On one occasion, seeing Frederick strolling through St James's Park, she declared: 'Look, there he goes – that wretch! – that villain! – I wish the ground would open this moment and sink the monster to the lowest hole in hell!'

In 1737, Caroline suffered an internal rupture. Her surgeon John Rainby – a man 'harsh of voice with inelegant manners' (inelegant manners not being the half of it, as we shall see) – was summoned. Caroline was fond of Rainby, or at least she was familiar enough with him to routinely address him as 'Blockhead'.

Caroline to Rainby:	'I am sure now, Blockhead, you are telling the King I have a rupture.'
Rainby to Queen Caroline:	'I am so, and there is no more time to be lost – your Majesty has concealed it for too long already.'

She would not conceal it for much longer. But despite her sufferings, Caroline retained that delightful sense of humour with which one will always associate the English aristocracy. When a visiting surgeon, bending to tend to the queen's needs, inadvertently brushed a lit candle and set his wig on fire, the queen begged Rainby to hold her hand, so that she could laugh.

Five days before her death, the queen's intestine ruptured completely. It was reported that 'the putrefying contents of her belly soaked through the sheets and over the floor'. The incident provoked a merciless couplet from Alexander Pope:

Here lies, wrapped in forty thousand towels,
The only proof that Caroline had bowels.

Charming.

The surgeon John Rainby is deserving of a closer look. For all his coarseness, he nevertheless moved in circles of high culture. He was on good terms with William Hogarth, and sat for the figure of Tom Rakewell in *A Rake's Progress*; he had accompanied George II as sergeant-surgeon at Dettingen. In 1745, he was elected as the Master of the Company of Surgeons.

But back to those 'inelegant manners'. Here's a rather chilling analysis of his character by a professional rival, the splendidly named Messenger Monsey: 'Rainby was the only man I ever heard coolly defend the use of laudanum in effecting his designs on women, which he confessed he had practised with success.' Rainby countered this distasteful allegation not with a rebuttal but with a crisp *ad hominem* swipe: Monsey, he said, was 'a nasty dog in a dirty shirt'.

Rainby's pal Hogarth was instrumental in cementing in the public mind the enduring association between Georgian London and gin.[6]

The London 'gin craze' gripped the city – or at least its poorer districts – between 1720 and 1751. Anti-gin ~~party-poopers~~ reformers did exaggerate the effects of the demon drink, blaming the drink known as 'geneve' for everything from poverty and disease to idleness and casual sex, but there's really no doubt that the people of London spent a large part of the eighteenth century on a truly colossal rout.

In 1737, there were around 8,659 'brandy shops' in London (against a paltry 6,000 alehouses). You didn't have to go to a shop for your snifter, though; you could buy cheap gin ('drunk for a penny, dead drunk for two!') in people's cellars and garrets, by the roadside, from dodgy geezers with wheelbarrows – pretty much anywhere you liked. In the slums of St Giles, one in four houses was a gin shop of some sort.

The Gin Act of 1751, which imposed stringent restrictions on the sale of the drink, reduced England's gin intake

to 2 million gallons a year. That might sound quite a lot, but before the Act was passed, the figure was up around 8 million gallons.

The thing about the cut-price gin swilling around the hovels and rat runs of Georgian London was that, quite often, it wasn't gin at all. Unscrupulous distillers would bulk out their 'gin' by cutting raw spirit with turpentine or sulphuric acid (mm, tangy).

These practices weren't restricted to gin, though: bread was stuffed with chalk and alum, wine fortified with zinc and arsenic compounds, tea-leaves replaced with the leaves of ash or elder trees. Nor were they restricted to the eighteenth century. In Victorian England, penny-pinching grocers were still putting strychnine in their beer, bisulphate of mercury in their chocolate, red lead in their cheese and chalk in their milk. One study of ice cream sold on the streets of nineteenth-century London found that the 'hokey-pokey', as it was known, contained 'cocci, bacilli, torulae, cotton fiber, lice, bed bugs, bugs' legs, fleas, straw, human hair, and cat and dog hair'.

You wouldn't get that sort of thing happening in our supermarkets nowadays, and anyone who says you would is talking ~~horsemeat~~ hogwash.

Shakespeare was dead, to begin with.[7] But in the 1740s one man brought him – figuratively speaking – back to life. When David Garrick was born in 1717, the Bard had been dead for 101 years, but that didn't stop the two of them forging a groundbreaking artistic partnership.

Garrick was a complete unknown when, in 1741, he played Shakespeare's Richard III on stage and took the theatrical world by storm. Audiences were sick of the stiff, pompous style adopted by most actors of the day; the tubby, sprightly little newcomer changed everything by – gasp! – trying to act like a real person.

He ended up playing seventeen different Shakespearean parts. He also produced twenty-four of Shakespeare's plays (and even went so far as to rewrite some of them, which goes to show that, even back then, great actors had great egos).

King George III (son of the 'wretched' and 'villainous' Frederick) succeeded his grandfather in 1760. No sooner was he on the throne than he was plunged into a swirl of political infighting, bloody foreign wars – and insolent requests from wig-makers.

The peruke industry – like the wool trade before it – had fallen on hard times. No one was wearing perukes (small gentlemen's wigs) any more. In 1764, the Company of Barbers and Peruke Makers went directly to the king to plead for royal intervention in the matter; in effect, asking George to play Cnut against the tide of changing fashions.

The penurious wig-mongers wailed:

As the Fashion your Majesty approves will very justly be a pattern to your subjects, We most humbly hope not to be too bold in wishing Perukes may soon be as much in fashion as the wearing of hair is at present, which will increase the Revenue, give happiness to the indigent and distressed Peruke makers, and increase the many great unmerited Favours, We as a Company have received from Royal Hands!

The king did not intervene. The peruke-makers remained indigent and distressed.

The enthusiastic sacking of John of Gaunt's Savoy Palace back in 1381 taught us that no one likes an *éminence grise*. In the 1760s, the power behind George III's throne was the Earl of Bute – and he attracted the sort of intense public loathing seldom seen since Gaunt was in his pomp. For one thing, Bute was Scottish. Being Scottish, in the 1760s, was the new being French.

But the young king would have been lost without him. 'In what a pretty pickle I should be in a future day if I had not your sagacious councils,' George wrote to Bute. No matter was too small to be submitted to the earl's judgment. In 1759, on entering the Lords, an anxious George wrote: 'I am desirous to know whether I am not to put on my hat on taking my seat.'

On 2 August, 1786, Margaret Nicholson ('a woman very decently dressed') attacked the king with an ivory-handled dessert knife. 'I am not hurt,' George said. 'Take care of the woman; do not hurt her, for she is mad.'

Given the mental illness that would soon overwhelm the king, the words have a great deal of poignancy.

Margaret Nicholson was a woman with a grievance. She was, she said, the rightful ruler of England; if she was not crowned queen, she warned, 'England would drown in blood for a thousand generations'.

You can probably guess where Margaret wound up.

London's Bethlehem Hospital was founded in 1247 by the nobleman (and tax-dodging City politician) Simon FitzMary. Simon was a former Crusader who one night, lost in the dark and in grave peril in the vicinity of the town of Bethlehem, had been saved by a bright star that guided him back to camp. The miraculous star was later depicted on the crest of the Bethlehem Hospital.

Time and sloppy diction soon did its work on the sacred name of the Bethlehem Hospital. Before very long, Bethlehem had become Bedlam. The long, grim and largely shameful history of Bedlam is peopled with fascinating characters and

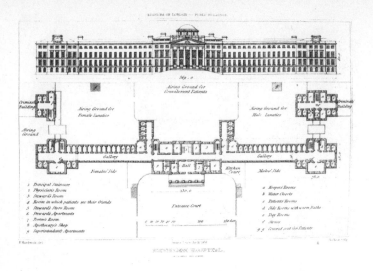

crowded with extraordinary stories. Few are as astonishing as
that of James Tilly Matthews, who was confined in Bedlam in
1796. He was kept there for the rest of his life.

Matthews claimed that he had been involved in covert
diplomacy with the Revolutionary government of France.
This – to some extent, at least – was true (although he didn't
have much luck with the French: they banged him up too).

He also believed that, from their lair in a London basement,
a cabal of shadowy revolutionaries was controlling the thoughts
and actions of the British government (and others) by means of
an Air Loom. The Loom was powered by 'seminal fluid, male and
female … effluvia of dogs – stinking human breath … stench of
the sesspool – gaz from the anus of a horse'. The Loom 'wove'
invisible airs and magnetic fluids into different configurations,
and then projected them on to unsuspecting subjects. Among
the miseries inflicted on Matthews (and others) by the Loom
were the processes of 'bomb bursting' – filling the stomach with
gas and then detonating it – and 'gaz-plucking' – the removal
of precious magnetic fluid, bubble by bubble, from the subject's
anus. This was probably not true.

He also, at times, believed himself to be the Emperor of the World, signing himself 'James, Absolute Sole and Sacred Omni Imperious Arch Grand Arch Sovereign Omni Imperious Arch Grand Arch Proprietor Omni Imperious Arch-Grand-Arch Emperor Supreme etc.' This was also probably not true.

In 1809, Dr Henry Clutterbuck examined Matthews. In evidence submitted to a habeas corpus hearing summoned to determine Matthews' state of mind, Clutterbuck reported that 'he could not discover any thing that indicated insanity in James Tilly Matthews and he verily believes him to be perfectly sane'.

From madness, we proceed to stupidity. The onset of the 1780s saw the emergence into public life of perhaps the most dangerous idiot the English aristocracy has yet produced.

George, Lord Gordon, was a former lieutenant in the Royal Navy. In the late 1770s he started to make a name for himself as an opponent of Catholic emancipation, and by 1780, he was obsessed by the issue. The MP Charles Turner observed that he 'had got a twist in his head, a certain whirligig which ran away with him if anything relative to religion was mentioned'.

The 'No Popery!' movement was built around opposition to the Catholic Relief Act (which really didn't give Catholics a great deal of relief at all). Gordon, as the movement's frothingly fanatical leader, soon amassed 44,000 signatures on a petition calling for the repeal of the Act. 'The conduct of Lord George,' the historian Earl Stanhope wrote, 'showed that he was well-entitled to his post of pre-eminence in folly'. During the parliamentary session of 1780, the same author adds, 'he made many speeches in the House of Commons, always marked by ignorant fanaticism, and often by low buffoonery'.

We are dealing here, it's clear, with one of English history's all-time cretins.

Gordon instructed his thousands of followers to assemble in St George's Fields on 2 June 1780, where he would present his petition to the government. A crowd of perhaps 60,000 duly assembled (their numbers swollen, Stanhope suggests, by 'the love of frolic and staring'). After George had given 'another of his silly speeches' (Stanhope again), the mob advanced on Parliament.

Numerous outrages were committed on the persons of several peers as they made their way through the hostile throng. Lord Mansfield, who was to preside over the day's proceedings, had his robe torn and his wig dishevelled, and took his seat 'quivering on the Woolsack[8] like an aspen', as the Duke of Gloucester put it; the Archbishop of York had his sleeves ripped off and thrown in his face; the Bishop of Lincoln was thrown from his carriage and forced to take refuge in a nearby house (from which he reputedly fled disguised in women's clothes), and Lord Boston only escaped having a crucifix carved into his forehead by engaging the mob in debate about whether the Pope was the Antichrist, and then making a run for it.

The debates that followed were the high point of the moronic Gordon's role in the riots that came to bear his name. As the Lords talked, Gordon kept the crowd outside updated with frequent shouted bulletins, such as 'Do you know that Lord North calls you a mob?' After being threatened with murder by Colonel Murray, however, he retired to the eating-room – and fell asleep.

In the days that followed, the mob – for a mob it certainly was – ran wild, far beyond the control of Gordon (or indeed of anyone else). Its slogan was still 'No Popery!' – but this really wasn't about the Catholic Relief Act any more. Churches were burned, houses sacked, shops pillaged, wine cellars drunk dry. Newgate Prison was stormed and the prisoners set free.

Not until 7 June was order restored: on King George's orders, the army was despatched into the streets of the city – and, with horrible loss of life by fire, drowning, drink and musket-shot, the riots came to an end. The death toll was perhaps 700. Ten times more property was destroyed in the Gordon Riots – in less than a week – than was destroyed in Paris during the French Revolution.

This was the period in which William Pitt the Younger rose to prominence. The son (as you may have guessed) of William Pitt the Elder, Pitt the Younger was Britain's youngest-ever prime minister when he moved into 10 Downing Street[9] in 1783. He was 24 years old.

He was known for his exceeding thinness, so the Georgian public – who loved a good pun – dubbed him 'Bottomless Pitt'.

'The learned pig was in his day a far greater object of admiration to the English nation than ever was Sir Isaac Newton,' the poet Robert Southey wrote in 1807. Newton certainly wouldn't have laughed at that – possibly because it was true.

The Learned Pig – or, to be precise, the original Learned Pig – was first exhibited in London in 1785. It's impossible to outdo the publicity bumf distributed at the time:

This entertaining and sagacious animal casts accounts by means of Typographical cards, in the same manner as a Printer composes, and by the same method sets down any capital or Surname, reckons the number of People present, tells by evoking on a Gentleman's Watch in company what is the Hour and Minutes; he likewise tells any Lady's Thoughts in company, and distinguishes all sorts of colours.

The Learned Pig was a smash hit. Numerous tribute acts followed. A 'Pig of Knowledge' was exhibited in New England. The illusionist Nicholas Hoare introduced 'Toby the Sapient Pig' to London audiences in the 1800s (and even published a spin-off book). William Pinchbeck had a Learned Pig that had been taught by 'Souchanguyee, the Chinese Philosopher'.

At Court, thoughts were turning to the Royal Succession. George III had always been deeply anxious – as monarchs generally are – about the production of an heir. When his queen Charlotte went into labour in August 1762, George let it be known that he would give £500 to whoever brought him news of a baby daughter – and £1,000 to whoever brought him news of a son.

The child was born at 7.24 p.m. on 12 August (a lady-in-waiting was taking careful notes). The Earl of Huntingdon, Master of the King's Horse, hastened to the king's chambers with the news – that the queen had given birth to a healthy baby daughter! Thus was the birth of the future George IV announced to the king. And thus did the ill-informed Huntingdon do himself out of 500 quid.

Such was the intrigue that often surrounded a royal birth – memories lingered of James II's 1688 'warming-pan' baby – that the Hanoverian administration went to great lengths to ensure that the legitimacy of this birth was in no doubt.

So, while George, the baby's father, was rightly and properly excluded from the birthing room, the queen endured her labour in the company of her German lady attendants and the Ladies of the Bedchamber – plus the First Lord of the Treasury, the two

Secretaries of State, the officers of the Privy Council, the officers of the Royal Household, and the Archbishop of Canterbury.

The boy – yet another George – was the couple's first child, and thus heir to the throne. George III definitely hadn't been married in secret to a Quaker girl called Hannah Lightfoot, the daughter of a Wapping shoemaker, many years before, and definitely hadn't had a child with her. If he had done, then it would mean that every single British monarch since 1820 was, technically, a usurper. But those things definitely didn't happen. So that's all right then.

In February 1789, George III pursued a best-selling lady novelist in a high-speed chase through Kew Gardens.

It shouldn't be necessary to add to this sensational statement, but a little background is probably required. George had been suffering from mental ill-health for some time; in the care of the formidable Lincolnshire specialist Francis Willis (and his equally formidable sons and attendants), he had been removed in November 1788 from Windsor to Kew.

The king wasn't always happy to comply with his doctor's orders (he was, after all, the king). On one day in January, Willis and his troop took George out for a pleasant stroll-cum-forced march in the gardens. But George was reluctant to go along with the plan: after a while, he sat down on the grass and refused to budge. Then he lay down on the grass. A passer-by, peeping over the wall, saw the king prostrate on the Kew lawn, and jumped to the obvious conclusion – that George was dead. 'And a report to this purpose,' the equerry Fulke Greville wrote, 'was soon spread over Kew and its neighbourhood!'

George was not dead, however. He was carried home lying horizontal on his attendants' shoulders. He then asked to be allowed to play a game of cards, but was instead strapped into a straitjacket.

And so to the lady novelist.

Frances Burney was one of the most celebrated female authors of her generation. She also attended on Queen Charlotte, consort of George III, at Kew in the 1780s. Burney seems to have been utterly terrified of the manic monarch. Knowing that a standing order was in place to keep out of George's way at all times, Burney was alarmed when she heard the king call out to her while she was walking in the gardens. Understandably, she legged it – but the king came after her.

It would all have been hilarious farce had George not been so bewildered and Burney not so petrified. 'I was ready to die,' she wrote. 'I do not think I should have felt the hot lava from Vesuvius … had I so run during its eruption. My feet were not sensible that they ever touched the ground.'

But eventually she was hunted down – his attendants, worried that the king was over-exerting himself, persuaded her at last to stop. She forced herself to face the wild-eyed king. He spread out his arms. 'I concluded he meant to crush me,' Burney wrote – but instead the king hugged her, and kissed her on the cheek.

Young George's relationship with Caroline of Brunswick started and ended in preposterous farce. Much of what went on in between was also preposterous farce. But let us begin at the beginning.

Prince George first met his future queen in April 1795, after she had been escorted to England by Sir James Harris, the Earl of Malmesbury. George greeted the princess politely, and then turned to Malmesbury.

'Harris,' he said, 'I am not well. Pray get me a glass of brandy.' Caroline, for her part, wasn't much impressed either. 'I find him very stout and by no means as handsome as his portrait,' she reported.

The pair were nevertheless married at St James's Palace on 8 April 1795. The altar was candlelit. A special anthem of rejoicing was sung. The bridegroom was thoroughly drunk. 'Not since the marriage of Henry VIII and Anne of Cleves,' one historian has written, 'had an English prince approached his nuptial bed with such antipathy.'

As in that case, one can hardly imagine that the bride was exactly jumping for joy either.

The first official disclosures of scandal within (or, rather, without) the royal marriage arose in 1806, when a royal commission was appointed to investigate the story of a young boy, William Austin, who, it was said, was Princess Caroline's son – and a possible future challenger for the throne.

The Commission conveniently found that the boy wasn't Caroline's – but that Caroline's behaviour in other respects (i.e. in respect of flirtatious shenanigans with various young officers) was 'liable to very unfavourable interpretations'. The multi-mistressed Prince George was, obviously, shocked by the revelations (the monstrous double standards can be taken as read).

In August 1814, Caroline, estranged from George, cleared off to mainland Europe, declaring that, as the English court would not give her the honours she deserved, she was content to remain 'Caroline, a happy merry soul'.

The adventures of happy merry Caroline as she spent the next six years romping across Europe are – alas – beyond the scope of this book (selected highlights included driving through Genoa at the age of 50 in a low-cut minidress and a pink feathered hat and turning up late to the opera in Baden dressed as an Alpine peasant). But she couldn't stay abroad forever; she was still married to the heir to the throne, and when, in 1820, Prince George became King George, Caroline instantly became the most embarrassing queen in English history.

Caroline duly returned to England for what was theatrically, if inaccurately, billed 'The Queen's Trial'. She was rapturously received and revelled in her popularity, yelling out a mocking 'Long live the king!' as her carriage swept by George's residence at Carlton House.

The 'trial' commenced in June 1820. Over eleven weeks, the details of her possibly adulterous dalliance with the Italian Bartolomeo Pergami were painstakingly teased out. Caroline, not permitted to give evidence, spent most of time playing backgammon in an adjoining room.

After one session, the Duke of Wellington – who had, remember, fought in the thick of the action on some of Europe's bloodiest battlefields – remarked: 'Never, in all my life, have I spent two more unpleasant hours.'

This long-running farce added greatly to the gaiety of the nation. The general public was largely on Team Caroline: one representative piece of graffiti read 'The Queen forever! The King in the river!'

The old (and sorrily deranged) King George III died on January 29. But no sooner had his son George IV come into his long-awaited inheritance than he very nearly went straight out of it. The longest-ever reign of an English king (George III's very-nearly sixty years) was a hair's breadth away from being followed by the shortest-ever.

On 31 January, the new king suffered an attack of pleurisy; by the night of 1 February, he was declared to be 'in imminent danger' of death. Approximately 150 fluid ounces of blood (about 4 litres, considerably more than an armful) was taken

from him by his doctors – he was too ill even to attend his father's funeral.

George's ill-health was unsurprising given his formidable stoutness, which was a continuing theme throughout his regency and reign. In 1813, at a 'Dandy Ball' given by Lord Alvanley, George haughtily 'cut' George 'Beau' Brummell, the famously dapper fop known for his stylish way with a stiffened cravat, not to mention a cutting one-liner. In response to the prince's snub, Brummell enquired loudly: 'Alvanley! Who's your fat friend?'

The remark caused more of a sensation than the stiffened cravat, and that's saying something – when Brummell debuted his unusually rigid neckwear, it was reported (perhaps mischievously) that 'its sensation was prodigious; dandies were stuck dumb with envy, and washerwomen miscarried'.

Obesity and gout in later life meant that George was unable to mount a horse without being wheeled up a ramp and hoisted into the saddle from a high platform. The many satirists of late Georgian England had a field day, the cruel beasts.

George was a man of many interests. One of the most endearing of these was his passion for Scotland – or, in any case, for what he imagined Scotland to be. George declared: 'I dislike seeing anything in Scotland that is not purely national and characteristic.' In effect, this made George IV the patron saint of the tartan-and-shortbread industry.

At Christmas 1811, George set out to demonstrate to his daughter, Princess Charlotte, the proper execution of a Highland fling. He landed heavily on his ankle, and was confined to bed for a fortnight afterwards (his brother, Ernest Augustus, remarked sourly that the poultice should be applied to George's head, rather than his ankle).

In July 1822, George, now king, took his Caledoniaphilia to another level, and announced that he would, that summer, visit Scotland in person. The novelist Sir Walter Scott (who, by the by, once described Caroline as 'that Bedlam Bitch of a Queen') was charged with choreographing the pageant.

Against all the odds, this first trip north of the border for a Hanoverian monarch was a roaring success. Although what the Scottish public made of the grossly overweight George kitted out in full Highland regalia – plus a pair of pink tights, for decency's sake – is anyone's guess. George's popularity in Scotland was even more surprising, given that he was the godson and great-nephew of the Duke of Cumberland, the infamous Butcher of Culloden.

It wouldn't be right to dwell for too long on the peculiarities of Prince George and his wife. If we do that, we won't have time to dwell on the peculiarities of his brothers.

Prince Edward, Duke of Kent, was a bullying martinet who had single-handedly sparked off a mutiny in Gibraltar through his 'disciplinary excesses' and had to be 'retired' from his post. Prince Ernest Augustus, Duke of Cumberland, known as 'the Black Sheep', was widely believed to be a murderer and an incestuous sexual pervert – though he later showed his willingness to conform to royal norms by marrying his cousin. Prince Adolphus, Duke of Cambridge, had a jolly habit of heckling preachers in church (he seems to have had difficulty in grasping the principle of a rhetorical question). And Prince William, Duke of Clarence, despite a lusty penchant for 'the pretty girls of Westminster' in his youth, settled down in 1790 to have ten children with his mistress, the famous actress Dorothy Bland (better known by her stage-name 'Mrs Dorothy Jordan').

We let this last one be king. He was crowned William IV in 1830.

But we aren't yet done with the excitements of the Georgian age.

In 1812, Spencer Perceval became the first British prime minister to be assassinated. A 'man in a green coat' – later identified as merchant-with-a-grudge Henry Bellingham – shot him dead in the lobby of the Commons. Bellingham was described as 'an alleged lunatic', but the authorities weren't having any of that – Bellingham was to hang.

Bellingham was accompanied to the gallows by a cheering crowd; though seemingly a decent man, Perceval, it's fair to say, had not been a popular prime minister. One commentator summed up the crowd's feeling thus: 'God bless you! you have rendered an important service to your country; you have taught ministers that they should do justice.'

The careers of Perceval's sons provide a curious postscript to this tragic affair. Spencer Perceval Jr, an MP, apparently went mad in the House of Commons on 20 March 1832. His bizarre rant began: 'Will ye not listen for a few moments to one who speaketh in the name of the Lord? I stand here to warn you of the righteous judgment of God, which is coming on you, and which is now near at hand!' and continued unstoppably in the same vein for some time. Hansard reported that 'indescribable confusion prevailed during great part of the hon. Gentleman's speech': 'Several Members surrounded Mr Perceval, and … requested him to desist from his extraordinary mode of proceeding; but Mr. Perceval proceeded.'

His brother John, meanwhile, had a breakdown of his own in 1831 – and later founded the Lunatics' Friendly Society.

Being prime minister has always been a very stressful job. None found it more so than Tory Henry Addington, 1st Viscount Sidmouth, who took on the post for a three-year stint in 1801. Before very long, his biographer notes, he was 'reduced to drinking perhaps twenty glasses of wine at dinner to invigorate himself for debate'.

Up until the 1800s, gas was known mostly as a thing to steer clear of if you were down a mine. Miners were uncomfortably aware that the stuff they called 'fire damp' combined with a naked flame was a recipe for an explosion. Explosions down mines seldom end happily. Gas, in short, was deadly.

But then, a factory hand called William Murdoch had the crackpot idea of deliberately setting fire to coal gas. He used it to light up his little house in Cornwall. To everyone's surprise, the little house in Cornwall wasn't blown to bits, and the idea started to catch on.

In 1807, Pall Mall was lit with gas lamps to celebrate the 69th birthday of George III (not that poor George, by this stage, was in any state to appreciate the gesture). Pall Mall was best known for its array of gouty old-fashioned gentlemen's clubs, but on 28 January, it became London's first gas-lit street and a gleaming beacon of hi-tech modernity – a development that surely had many a ruddy-faced member of the Athenaeum or the Reform Club choking indignantly on his port.

The story of how England defeated Napoleon (and then accidentally let him go, and then, once he and his men were knackered and half-dead from hunger and cold, defeated him again) is enough to stir any patriotic heart.

But we might not have beaten him at all, had Lady Catherine Sarah Dorothea Pakenham not been so choosy in the matter of future husbands. This was the love-affair that changed the face of European history. When his offer of marriage was turned down by Lady Catherine in 1793, the young musician Arthur Wellesley burnt his violin, and vowed to concentrate on a military career instead. By 1814, his glittering and bloodstained career as a soldier had earned him worldwide fame, and a title: the Duke of Wellington.

Wellington's predecessor as England's greatest military hero also narrowly avoided a terrible fate at the start of his career. Young Horatio Nelson was on a voyage to the Arctic Circle when he went for an unauthorised off-ship wander – and was almost killed by a polar bear.

Napoleon famously wished for 'lucky generals'. In that case, he wouldn't have wanted Lord Nelson anywhere near his army.

Shortly after the aforementioned polar bear attack, Nelson was laid low by a life-threatening illness. Having recovered, he shipped out to Central America, where he was laid low by a life-threatening tropical fever. Four years later he was struck in the face by stones thrown up by enemy fire, and lost the sight in his right eye. At Santa Cruz in 1797, he lost his arm. In 1798, he was wounded in the head and severely concussed. At the end of 1804 he fell ill. Finally, on 21 September 1805, at Trafalgar, he was shot through the shoulder and lung by a musket-ball.

Of course, if a chap is going to insist on being staggeringly brave and daring, these things will happen. That final musket ball, of course, killed Nelson, at the age of 47. He was preserved in a barrel of spirits, and brought home.

The Battle of Waterloo, on 18 June 1815, was a truly brutal day's fighting. Such was the strain put on Wellington's men – and the honour accorded them afterwards – that, for the purposes of calculating a soldier's pension, a single day's service at Waterloo counted as two years.

The final defeat of Boney was a great victory, of course – but was it a great British victory? Once again, it depends what you mean by 'British'. Less than half of Wellington's army at Waterloo were actually British; the rest were German, Belgian and Dutch.

Waterloo was the setting for one of the most famously stiff-upper-lipped conversations in English military history. Cavalry commander Henry Paget, the 2nd Earl of Uxbridge, was positioned near the Duke of Wellington when he was struck by a French cannonball.

'By God, sir, I've lost my leg!' Uxbridge remarked.

'By God, sir, so you have!' Wellington replied.

But this famous exchange is not, amazingly, the best example of officer-class stoicism to have emerged from the carnage of Waterloo.

Early in the evening of 18 June, a young English officer entered the field hospital a little way behind the Allied line. He was Lord Fitzroy Somerset, Wellington's chief aide-de-camp, and his right arm had been shattered by a sniper's bullet. The surgeon, no doubt somewhat wearily, picked up his saw.

Fitzroy, pinned down by the surgeon's assistants, made no sound as his arm was methodically sawn off between his shoulder and elbow. Only when the surgeon tossed the severed limb aside did the young officer speak up. 'Hey, bring back my arm,' he called. 'There's a ring my wife gave me on the finger.'

Fitzroy went on to become Lord Raglan, best known for making a colossal hash of the Battle of Balaklava thirty-nine years later. But we'll come to that in due course.

or, Everything You Always Wanted to Know About
Saxe-Coburg-Gotha But Were Afraid to Ask

Queen Victoria arrived on the throne in 1838. Much is sometimes made of the Germanic character of Victoria's household – she was half-German on her mother's side, she married a German (Prince Albert), spoke German with him at home, and even, according to some accounts, spoke with a German accent – but, by the standards of England's monarchs, she was still above average, Englishness-wise.

Victoria was a very tiny queen: she peaked at 4ft 11in, and got shorter as she got older. After her marriage, she was content to remain in her husband's shadow figuratively as well as literally: Albert, she believed, was 'the perfect being'. Therefore in 1851, when Victoria and Albert dutifully filled out their census form, they listed Albert as the 'Head of the Household'. Further down the list came Victoria – occupation, 'The Queen'.

Pregnancy was pretty much a way of life for Victoria. She had her first child in 1840 and her last in 1857, and found time to have seven more in-between. Her first pregnancy was not, it seems, much fun. 'If I have a nasty girl at the end of my plagues,' she wrote while expecting her first child, 'I shall drown it!'

She did have a girl. She didn't drown it. She called it Victoria instead. Princess 'Vicky', happily, was adored by both her parents (and, to her disappointed attendants at court, the queen said cheerfully: 'Never mind, the next will be a prince' – and she was right).

During the birth of Leopold, her eighth child, Victoria's personal physician, John Snow, administered a cutting-edge new super-drug designed to numb pain. It was known as 'chloroform'. The queen liked it: it was 'soothing, quieting & delightful beyond measure,' she reported. The medical establishment, suspicious of the new drug, was less enthused, however. *The Lancet* described the event as a 'deplorable catastrophe'.

In the first decade of the Victorian era, seventy-nine lives were lost in one of English history's strangest disasters. It wasn't so much the disaster itself that was peculiar – a suspension bridge in Great Yarmouth collapsed into the River Bure – but the reason why so many people were assembled on the bridge in the first place.

They were there to see a celebrity. Nelson the Clown, of William Cooke's Circus, had announced (with great fanfare) that he was to sail up the river in a barrel pulled by four geese. Around 350 spectators, straining for a view of the goose-drawn clown, were gathered on the bridge when it gave way.

One of the iconic events of Victoria's reign was the instalment of Big Ben in the tower of the Houses of Parliament. Big Ben is the successor of the Parliamentary bell known as Great Edward or Great Tom that had chimed the hour in the days of Edward I.

We're not sure who Edward or Tom were and we don't really know who Ben was, either. He might have been 'Big' Ben Caunt, a bareknuckle boxer from the days when a boxing match could last for over 100 rounds (of Caunt's 101-round fight with 'Brassey' Leechman in 1840, one journalist wrote: 'We have seldom recorded a fight in which we experienced more difficulty to render the details interesting'; of Caunt himself a critic wrote 'he hits at random and has no idea of self-defence'). More boringly but more probably, 'Big Ben' was Sir Benjamin Hall, the First Commissioner for Works.

The bell 'Big Ben' first rang out on 11 July 1859. In September 1859, it cracked. Big Ben was silent for four years. Another triumph for British craftsmanship.

Parliament loves its history. What other institution would maintain to this day an eighteenth-century tradition of providing free snuff for MPs (though the Commons points out that 'very few Members take snuff nowadays')?[10] Where else would employees be forbidden to address their colleagues while wearing a hat, unless they are lucky enough to be female? Where else would it be necessary to have a rule that prohibits the wearing of armour in the House (that one goes back to 1313, and Edward II)?

The custom-crazy Commons voted in 1999 to maintain yet another venerable tradition: that of printing new Acts of Parliament on 'vellum' or goatskin (at a cost of £30,000 a year). The oldest goatskin Acts in England date back to the late 1400s. A resolution passed in 1849 made it an official requirement that two copies of each Act be printed on goatskin.

One of the main reasons given in 1999 for maintaining the tradition was the need to support England's ancient vellum-printing industry – an industry that, at the time of the vote, employed only twelve people.

There has always been more to English industry, of course, than goatskin and badly cast giant bells. English industry was the engine of the British Empire, and England the cradle of an industrial revolution that transformed the world. The men behind this revolution were true giants, true geniuses, and in many cases truly peculiar.

The greatest of all – not just of industrialists and engineers but, by many estimates, of all Britons – was Isambard Kingdom Brunel.

Brunel's most fascinating construction was not the SS *Great Britain* or the Clifton Suspension Bridge or the Great Western Railway (though construction on it began, as with the railway, in 1833). It was a plank, fastened to a pivot. You see, Brunel had swallowed a half-sovereign. Alarmingly, it had gone the way of his lungs rather than his stomach. After two days of suffering, the great engineer had had enough. The plank was fastened to the pivot, and Brunel was strapped to the plank. The device was used to tilt Brunel (presumably minus his stovepipe hat and cigar) upside-down. He was then slapped vigorously on the back.

This ingenious cure for half-sovereign-swallowing was Brunel's own invention. Unlike most of his inventions, however, it didn't work. It produced a fit of choking, it's true – but no coin.

One failure wasn't enough to deter a can-do man like Brunel. Three and a half weeks later, he tried again – and failed again. The coin was dislodged, but not far enough. A surgical attempt to get at the coin by cutting open Brunel's windpipe also proved fruitless. After another fortnight – after having had a coin in his lung for more than a month – he once again endured the upside-down slapping treatment. The coin popped from his mouth. Brunel was saved – and ten shillings richer.

We all know the old Yorkshire saying, 'Where there's alpacas, there's brass.' Titus Salt certainly did. Yorkshireman Salt was one of the great Victorian industrialists. He made his fortune in the 1830s by exploiting a resource others overlooked – not scrap or waste or manure, but the wool of the llama-like alpaca.

Alpaca wool, everyone thought, was useless for manufacturing. It was imported to England, from the alpacas' South American homeland, but only because it served well as ballast in ships carrying far more valuable cargo.

Working in secret, Salt figured out how to transform this alpaca-wool into ladieswear – and made a killing. This is why Saltaire, the Yorkshire village Salt built for his mill workers (and modestly named after himself), is gratefully festooned with statues and engravings of alpacas.

Salt was a considerate employer by the standards of his day, and his vast Saltaire mill was a modern industrial wonder. But he was also a bossy so-and-so. The workers of Saltaire were left in no doubt as to who was in charge.

Among the rules imposed by Salt on his employees between 1853 and 1876 were that 'throughout the village, cleanliness, cheerfulness, and order must reign supreme'; that 'anyone caught in a state of inebriation will immediately be evicted'; that 'no washing [is] to be hung out to dry in front or behind any of the properties'; and that 'gatherings or loitering of more than eight persons in the streets is strictly forbidden'. Moreover, Titus 'recommended' that 'all inmates wash themselves every morning' – but 'they shall wash themselves at least twice a week, Monday morning and Thursday morning; any found not washed will be fined 3*d* for each offence'.

In the 1850s, a rather obscure and confused conflict broke out on the shores of the Black Sea, on the peninsula known as the Crimea. Soon, without really understanding what on earth was going on over there except that the Russians were being fiendish in some unspecified way, England had gone Crimea-crazy.

Such was the craze for anything Crimean that 'Florence' (after saintly nurse Nightingale) became a popular girl's name, as did 'Alma' and – less expectedly – 'Balaklava' (both after battles). In the same vein, many unfortunate boys were saddled with the name 'Inkerman'.

You might have thought that a far-off war in which 4,000 men died of wounds and 19,000 more died of disease wouldn't be the sort of thing you'd want to name a baby after, but, by Victorian lights, you'd be wrong.

★DEBUNKING KLAXON★

The Victoria Cross, Britain's highest military honour, was instituted in the queen's name in 1857 in order to honour the courage of those who performed deeds of extraordinary valour in the Crimea. It is generally maintained that the medals were cast in bronze from melted-down cannons captured following the Siege of Sevastopol in 1854–55.

It's the sort of claim you might expect to hear from a shifty online souvenir trader, and, as in that instance, caution and due diligence is required. When historians actually looked into the provenance of the first VC medals, they were found to have come, not from Sevastopol or indeed from anywhere in the Crimea, but from antique Chinese guns.

There is one particular solace in which the embattled English soldier has traditionally taken comfort during times of hardship. And we're not talking about religion.

During the Crimean War, a staggering 5,546 British soldiers were court-martialled for acts of drunkenness. Staff Officer Henry Clifford reported seeing English soldiers in the Crimea 'in every state of intoxication. Merry, laughing, crying, fighting, sentimental, affectionate, singing, talking, quarrelsome, stupid, beastly, brutal and dead-drunk.' 'What a mistake to over-pay a soldier!' he added. 'Let him be English, French, Turk, Sardinian, give him enough money and he will get drunk.'

The Crimea was hardly unique in this regard. At Waterloo, the British army had been more or less sozzled on gin throughout; one square of infrantrymen even broke open and drank a barrel of spirits while the battle was going on. And at Agincourt, too, there had been many a pre-battle snifter: 'It is quite probable that many soldiers in both armies went into the mêlée less than sober, if not fighting drunk,' one historian has concluded.

The British officers in the Crimea didn't go out of their way to ease the discomfort of their men (who were generally either hungry, cold, hot, diseased, being shot at or some combination of all five). In addition to their military duties, they were given the added burden of having to shave every day – no easy task with a hangover.

In the early months of the war, Commander-in-Chief Lord Raglan (he of the amputated arm) imposed a strict no-beards policy. 'I cling to the desire that an Englishman should look like an Englishman,' he wrote.

Not everyone in the military establishment was as obsessed with tradition as Raglan. The Royal Navy, for instance, saw the havoc that had been wrought in the Crimea by steam-powered warships and, instead of thinking, 'How perfectly vulgar!' simply thought 'Wow.'

Almost at once, the navy's sailing ships were obsolete. In a huge technological leap, the *Warrior*, England's first ironclad steamship, was born. It was as though the RAF had leapt straight from the Sopwith Camel to the supersonic Tornado G4 without bothering with any of the bits in between.

Seeing the *Warrior* sitting among the old man-o'-wars in Portsmouth harbour, Viscount Palmerston likened her to 'a snake among the rabbits'.[11]

Henry John Temple, the 3rd Viscount Palmerston and prime minister from 1855 to 1858 (and again from '59 to '65), was nicknamed 'The Mongoose' (for his tenacity) or, punningly, 'Lord Pumice-stone'. He was a brilliant orator and an indefatigable womaniser – hence his other nickname, 'Lord Cupid'. He recorded his sexual successes (and, very fair-mindedly, his failures) in pocket notebooks. He married his mistress – once described as 'one of the most profligate women in London' – in 1839 (pretty much as soon as her husband died).

After a famous speech in Parliament in 1850, in which he thundered for four and a half hours about how 'a British subject, in whatever land he may be, shall feel confident that the watchful eye and the strong arm of England will protect him against injustice and wrong', and so on, the 66-year-old Palmerston climbed up into the public gallery to give his wife a kiss. Palmerston was the last British prime minister to die in office.

In 1859, Charles Darwin changed the world. Without *On the Origin of Species* and Darwin's theory of evolution by natural selection, our understanding of how the natural world works (and how we fit into it) would have remained mired in dogma and ignorance – and Darwin would be remembered as little more than a first-rate barnacles man.

The minutiae of barnacle life occupied the insatiably curious Darwin for years. His barnacle studies were a fundamental part

of life in the Darwin household – so much so that when William, Darwin's young son, visited a friend's house, he innocently asked: 'And where does your father do his barnacles?'

Elsewhere in the nineteenth century, a sinister man nicknamed Jack haunted the streets of south-east London, striking fear into the hearts of vulnerable young women. No, not him – we'll come to him later. This Jack never killed anyone – but by 1838 he had, according to a letter sent to the Mayor of London, 'succeeded in depriving seven ladies of their sense'.

This was Spring-heeled Jack, a sinister figure who, in February 1838, set upon 18-year-old Jane Alsop, 'vomit[ing] forth a quantity of blue and white flames from his mouth' and '[tearing] at her neck and arms with his claws'. The main suspect was a drunken carpenter named Millbank, which seems odd, given that carpenters, drunken or sober, are not known for their fire-breathing capabilities (or their claws, come to that). Hysteria followed. 'Jack' was reportedly seen (often vomiting flames) in more than thirty locations around the city.

The bizarre prankster, whoever he was, ceased his infernal pestering after 1838 – but he lived on in legend, the subject of spooky yarns (and unit-shifting media attention) as far afield as Aldershot and Sheffield. The last reports of 'Spring-heeled Jack' arose in 1904, in Liverpool.

***

One of the main suspects in the Spring-heeled Jack scare was Henry Beresford, the 3rd Marquess of Waterford. Even if he wasn't Jack, he's worth taking a look at anyway, because for many years he was the country's most notorious 'young blood'.[12]

The Eton and Oxford-educated Waterford had the sort of highly developed sense of humour that only years of elite schooling can provide; among his chief entertainments were breaking windows, overturning market-stalls and starting fights. On one memorable occasion, he painted the heels of a parson's horse with aniseed, and hunted him with bloodhounds.

Amazingly, this braying hooray was reformed by his marriage in 1842 to the beautiful and refined Louisa Stuart. He still went hunting six days a week, though (just not after parsons, or at least not always). He died on the hunting field, of a broken neck, at the age of 48.

Now, on to that other Jack – the really unpleasant one. There's no need to delve into the spectacularly grim details of the Ripper killings of the 1880s – but we can take a look at who might have been responsible for them.

Among the suspects are (deep breath): Montague John Druitt, Seweryn Kłosowski (alias George Chapman), Aaron Kosminski, Michael Ostrog, John Pizer, James Thomas Sadler, Francis Tumblety, William Henry Bury, Thomas Neill Cream, Thomas Hayne Cutbush, Frederick Bailey Deeming, Carl Feigenbaum, Robert Donston Stephenson, Joseph Barnett, David Cohen, William Withey Gull, George Hutchinson, James Kelly, James Maybrick, Alexander Pedachenko, Walter Sickert, Joseph Silver, James Kenneth Stephen, Francis Thompson, Sir John Williams, Prince Albert Victor, Duke of Clarence, Uncle Tom Cobleigh, and all.

That's only a selection. The complete list of possible Rippers stretches to over 130 names. Of course, some of these are what we in the history business call 'just silly'. But the range of suspects – some taken seriously by the police at the time, others dreamed up or discovered later by researchers – gives us an indication of just how little we know about Jack the Ripper.

'Jack the Ripper' probably wasn't even his real pseudonym. The September 1888 letter signed with that name was, in all likelihood, a hoax cooked up by the press.

But the killings – at least five, and perhaps more – were real enough.

Alright: one spectacularly grim detail – in the context of one eyebrow-raising coincidence. The Ripper's third victim, Elizabeth Stride, lived with a local docker named

Michael Kidney. The fourth victim, Catherine Eddowes, was murdered almost immediately afterwards – and her kidney was sent in a parcel to the Mile End Vigilance Committee.

Ghastly murders of this sort were the bread-and-butter of the Victorian popular press – and the Victorian public lapped it up.

Even thoroughly respectable sorts couldn't get enough of it. For example, Philip Henry Gosse, a marine biologist and a fundamentalist Christian with a decided hellfire bent, was in the habit not only of reading these gruesome gutter-press reports, but of sharing them with his young son. In his book *Father and Son*, the son – Edmund Gosse – gives a strangely touching account of how the pair whiled away dark evenings discussing 'our favourite subject' – murder. 'I wonder whether little boys of eight, soon to go upstairs alone at night, often discuss violent crime with a widower-papa?' Gosse wonders. 'The practice, I cannot help thinking, is unusual.'

The boy Gosse was thrilled by stories of the Edinburgh murderers Burke and Hare and of Mrs Manning, who 'killed a gentleman on the stairs and buried him in quick-lime in the back-kitchen' (Mrs Manning, Gosse adds in a 'useful historical fact', was hanged in black satin, which thereupon 'went wholly out of fashion in England').

Most compelling of all was a macabre tale that was subsequently to mystify Gosse: the 'Carpet-bag Mystery'. This case, of human remains found bundled in a carpet bag and suspended from Waterloo Bridge, was not, it seems, well-remembered in 1907, when Gosse published his memoir: 'Who will tell me what the "Carpet-bag Mystery" was, which my Father and I discussed evening after evening? I have never come across a whisper of it since, and I suspect it of having been a hoax.'

It was no hoax.

EXECUTION OF WILLIAM BURKE.
(From a Contemporary Print.)

On 10 October 1857 – Gosse would indeed have been 8 – some boys boating on the Thames found a carpet-bag on a bridge abutment. Inside were twenty-three human bones (what Gosse called 'a dreadful butcher's business of joints and fragments') and a suit of bloodsoaked clothing. Inevitably, public speculation focused on two groups of highly suspect individuals: surgeons, and foreigners. But no bodysnatching sawbones or swarthy French spy was ever hauled in to Bow Street Station to answer for the crime – in spite of a £300 reward. So no hoax, then – but certainly a (still unsolved) mystery.

Electric taxis are smaller, cleaner and less noisy than the existing alternatives – and, unlike the existing alternatives, they're not likely to do a poo in the road. This is not a slur on the personal hygiene of today's black-cab drivers, but, rather, is the argument put forward in the 1890s when an exciting new technology, the 'Bersey' electric cab, arrived on London's horse-manure-strewn streets.

The softly murmuring Berseys were nicknamed 'Hummingbirds' (or, more likely, ''Ummingbirds', because this is Cockneys we're talkin' abaat). But, though well-liked, the Berseys didn't last long. Petrol-powered taxis arrived in 1903, and were far more reliable. Yes, they generated a choking stink and billowing clouds of carbon, but that was never going to have any long-term consequences, now was it.

The Victorian era came to a close with a war that, like that fought in the Crimea forty-odd years before, got everybody very excited but ended with nothing much to cheer about at all. The Boer War was a miserable colonial scrap that happened to cost Britain in excess of £200 million, more than any other conflict between 1815 and 1914.

or, When We Were Very Young

In the summer of 1912, England had a foretaste of tragedy when Captain Scott and four of his men perished in the snows of Antarctica after failing to beat the Norwegian Roald Amundsen to the South Pole (although actually, to be strictly accurate, England didn't know a thing about it until February 1913, when the first reports hit the newsstands).

For most of Scott's journeys in Antarctica, he and his men hauled their own sleds. It was such hot and heavy work that, on several occasions, they did so in their underwear. On other occasions conditions were rather less clement. Apsley Cherry-Garrard, a member of Scott's team but not part of the polar party, described weather so cold (around –51 °C) that men's teeth cracked. Cherry-Garrard's book about the expedition was entitled *The Worst Journey in The World* – but the title didn't

refer to the trek that killed Scott and his comrades. Instead, it described the long march made in the sunless Antarctic winter by Cherry-Garrard and two other men (but not Scott) to gather penguin eggs. Cherry-Garrard called it 'the weirdest bird-nesting expedition that has been or ever will be'.

Speaking of birds and untimely death, in 1913 Edward VII and his son, the future George V, set a British record for a day's 'bag' by killing 3,937 birds in a single day's shooting. 'Perhaps we overdid it today,' the king remarked afterwards.

It's thought that the career record is held by the second Marquess of Ripon, who bagged a total of 556,813 birds in his 'career'.[13]

The theme of heroic young men dying far from home was, of course, to be picked up again a couple of years later.

Mons was the first major battle of the First World War. By the time it was over, around 1,600 British soldiers were killed, injured or missing. But there was one more casualty still to come – 19-year-old Tom Highgate, who fled the battle to hide in a barn, and who two weeks later would be shot by his own side for desertion. There were no witnesses for the defence at his trial – because all of his comrades had been killed or captured.

It's often thought that Field Marshal Sir Douglas Haig, the supreme commander of the British Army in the First World War, was a haughty man, unwilling to listen to criticism or counsel. This is not true. As a younger man, Haig willingly sought the advice of a more experienced, older general. Ninety-two years older, to be precise; Haig's venerable counsellor was none other than Napoleon Bonaparte. Haig, a spiritualist as well as a religious fundamentalist, attended a number of séances – and at one was put in contact with the Little Corporal himself.

It's worth remembering, however, that Napoleon would not have been such a distant figure to Haig as he is to us. However modern the First World War sometimes seems, the Battle of the Somme was nearer in time to Napoleon's death (in 1821) than to us (and while we're at it, Agincourt was closer in time to Hastings than to Waterloo, and Hastings closer in time to the death of Marcus Aurelius than to us).

Time, in short, is a funny thing. Now back to the Front.

No goalposts – just army caps or tin helmets. And no ball, either – they used bundles of straw or empty boxes instead. Still, it was football, just about. And it was more fun than fighting.

On Christmas Eve 1914, a few months after the start of the First World War, the German, Austrian, French and English soldiers camped in the bleak trenches of the Western Front decided that Christmas was no time for warfare. It was a time for peace, friendship – and football. All along the 500 miles of trenches, impromptu kickabouts in 'no man's land' provided the men at the Front with a temporary break from the horrors of the war. In fact, the Christmas truce was so popular that some soldiers, to the horror of their commanding officers, didn't get back to the important business of shooting each other until several weeks later.

But not everyone enjoyed the holiday (which became known in German as Der Kleine Frieden, 'the little peace'). One young Austrian soldier complained that such high jinks 'should not be allowed'. His name was Lance-corporal Adolf Hitler.

Just as Churchill wasn't the only English PM to have seen the reality of war, Hitler was not the only future European leader to serve in the trenches. Harold Macmillan, prime minister from 1957 to 1963, was in fact a bona fide war hero.

In 1916, in the Battle of the Somme, Macmillan was severely wounded in the thigh and hip. He lay helpless in a shell-hole in no-man's-land for a day – and passed the time by reading the classical tragedian Aeschylus in the original Greek. This puts Macmillan firmly in the tradition of such highly educated PMs such as W.E. Gladstone, of whom Winston Churchill remarked: 'Mr Gladstone read Homer for fun, which I thought served him right.'[14]

There were many heroes away from the hardships of the Front, of course. Edith Cavell, for one.

Cavell was an English nurse stationed at a hospital in Brussels. Between autumn 1914 and summer 1915, Edith and a small group of fellow humanitarians helped more than 200 Allied soldiers to escape across the border into neutral Holland. In August 1915, though, she was arrested by the Germans. She confessed and was sentenced to death. Her words on the eve of her execution soon became well known. 'Patriotism is

EDITH CAVELL

not enough,' she declared. 'I must have no hatred or bitterness towards anyone.'

The German minister Baron Von de Landen, on the other hand, made his position on the matter quite clear. He would, he said, rather have Edith shot than have any harm come to a

German soldier – and that his only regret was that he did not have 'three or four English old women to shoot'.

Given the close ties of our royal family to the German aristocracy (Kaiser Wilhelm, for instance, was George V's first cousin), the First World War was fraught with upper-class awkwardness and embarrassment.

Some handled their conflicting loyalties better than others. Queen Victoria's grandson Prince Charles Edward, Duke of Saxe-Coburg and Gotha, handled them badly: in 1919, he was stripped of his titles for taking the Kaiser's side in the conflict – and later went on to join the Nazi Party.

Grand gestures aimed at expressing solidarity with those at the front were common during the First World War. George V, for instance, took 'the King's Pledge' – to abstain from alcohol for the duration of the conflict.

A later wartime leader would have struggled with such a challenge. In 1936, Winston Churchill refused a bet of £2,000 from Lord Beaverbrook that the soon-to-be PM couldn't

remain teetotal for a year. Churchill offered a less-demanding counter-wager: £600 that he could go a year without drinking any undiluted spirits.

Nancy Astor disliked drinking. She also disliked Winston Churchill. These two facts were not unrelated.[15]

Astor is well known as the first woman to be elected to the House of Commons. In fact she was no such thing: that honour went to Constance Markievicz in the General Election 1918, an achievement made all the more impressive by the fact that she was in prison at the time. Markievicz, London-born of Polish heritage, was an MP for the Irish Republican Party Sinn Féin. Like all Sinn Féin MPs, she declined to take an oath to the king – and thus forfeited her seat in the Commons.

Nancy Astor, taking her seat on 1 December 1919, was happy to swear the oath – despite having been born and raised in the US. Among Astor's notable achievements in office were an ill-fated attempt to convert Josef Stalin to Christian Science in 1934 and performing cartwheels to entertain sailors in Plymouth during the Blitz.

There may have been another 'first' in the decade after the war – another bold individual reaching previously unexplored new heights. The English climber George Mallory may have made it to the summit of Everest, nineteen years before Sir Edmund Hillary.[16] We don't know. All we know is that he never made it back down again.

The breathtakingly daring Mallory had already assured himself of a place in mountaineering history. While climbing Snowdon, he found that he had left his pipe on a ledge halfway down one of the precipices; he scrambled back by a short cut to retrieve it, then came back up by the same route. When the party came to examine the route the next day for the official record of the climb, they found an overhang nearly all the way. In breach of mountaineering protocol, which states that climbing routes can be named only after natural features and not after people, the climb was named in the young daredevil's honour. It was recorded as follows: 'Mallory's Pipe: a variation on Route 2 ... This climb is totally impossible. It has been performed once, in failing light, by Mr GHL Mallory.'

The tragic deaths of Mallory and his climbing partner Andrew Irvine on the mountain in 1924 made Everest famous.[17] It also, indirectly, caused a diplomatic breach with Tibet.

Photographer John Noel had led the campaign to raise funds for the 1924 expedition. Among his PR brainwaves was sending out postcards from Everest base camp: hundreds of people sent in their addresses in return for one of the cards (complete with specially printed Everest stamp).

After the expedition, as he toured the lecture circuit, Noel hit upon the idea of persuading a troupe of Tibetan Buddhist monks to perform traditional dances before each showing of his films from Everest. But the dances were supposed to be sacred – not promoted as a 'dancing lamas' show. The Tibetan authorities were not amused.

Another pair of brave English pioneers made headlines in the post-war years: John Alcock and Arthur Whitten Brown, who completed the first transatlantic flight in June 1919. The pair had both flown in the war (though both had been shot down, which didn't bode well).

The flight from America to Ireland was uneventful, unless you count the radio cutting out, the airspeed indicator breaking down, snow piling up in the cockpit, and Whitten Brown having to climb out on to the wings to clear away ice.

They landed in what had seemed from the air to be a lovely green field but was in fact a lovely green bog (in fairness, they had by this point been flying non-stop for sixteen hours and so probably weren't at their sharpest). They received a £10,000 prize from the *Daily Mail* for their achievement – but gave their first interview to the man from the *Connacht Tribune*. What a scoop!

***

Canada-born Andrew Bonar Law served as PM for just 209 days in 1922–23. On his burial in Westminster Abbey, former prime minister Herbert Asquith remarked that 'we have buried the Unknown prime minister by the side of the Unknown Soldier'.

He was not our only foreign-born PM. The Duke of Wellington was born in Dublin (while Ireland was a foreign country). Nor was his was the shortest term served by a PM: George Canning held the office for 119 days in 1827 (in fairness to Canning, he did have a good excuse for leaving Number 10 early – overworked and ill, he became one of only seven prime ministers to die in office).

***

In the summer of 1927, holidaymakers in the seaside town of Great Yarmouth may have seen a shifty-looking character with a hat and a pipe hanging around on the promenade.

Instead of giving the man a wide berth or passing his details on to the police, many approached him – and they all said the same thing: 'You are Mr Lobby Lud – I claim the *Westminster Gazette* prize.'

Mr Lobby Lud was in fact *Westminster Gazette* reporter Willy Chinn. The paper's marketing men had come up with the inspired idea of getting Chinn dressed up, putting his picture in the *Gazette*, and offering a prize of £50 to anyone who challenged him.

The stunt was a massive success. It almost caused a riot in Eastbourne, as fortune-hunters took to demanding £50 from anyone who wore a hat and smoked a pipe (in 1927, that was pretty much everybody). The uncontrolled Ludmania prompted one harassed Lobby-a-like to complain to the newspaper. 'Married life in these days is a big enough problem without being taken for Mr Lud,' he grumbled.

Winston Churchill was born at Blenheim Palace on 30 November 1874. His parents, Lord Randolph and Jennie Churchill, had been married seven-and-a-half months earlier. As one historian has discreetly put it, 'we must suspend judgment as to whether this was simply the first instance of Winston's impetuosity, or whether it involved yet another of Lord Randolph's'.

Winston himself inclined to the former view. He described Blenheim as the place where 'I took two important decisions: to be born and to marry'.

Churchill was bent on a military career – specifically, a glorious military career – from a very young age. He attributed this, not

to the martial accomplishments of his forefathers, but to the contents of his toy box: his military ambitions were, he said, 'entirely due to my collection of soldiers'. His collection, he added, was 'nearly fifteen hundred' strong.

While fighting alongside Lord Kitchener in the Sudan in 1898, Churchill was required to volunteer a piece of flesh from his forearm so that a comrade could receive a skin graft. The doctor responsible for the operation comfortingly explained to the young soldier that the procedure was 'like being flayed alive'.

It wasn't the last time Churchill voluntarily subjected his forearm to severe pain. He also had a tattoo there – of a Popeye-style anchor. This was in the best tradition of English war leaders: Harold II, for instance, had several tattoos, including the name of his wife, 'Edith', across his heart. After Hastings, the king's tats were used to help identify his body.

'MR CHURCHILL BREAKS DOWN', the news headlines read. 'MOVING INCIDENT IN THE HOUSE'.

Those fearing a Spencer Perceval Jr-style meltdown were soon reassured. Young Churchill – 'the new Tory bully' as the Liberal David Lloyd George had immediately dubbed him[18] – had simply forgotten, halfway through a speech in the Commons, what it was he had to say. It was with good reason that Churchill, in later life, would often quip that he was 'just preparing my impromptu remarks'.

The Second World War wrecked millions of lives and left Europe in ruins. Often overlooked, however, is the devastating effect it had on ladies' underwear.

In wartime England, rubber shortages meant that elastic knickers frequently gave way at inopportune moments. Often, the only possible response to unanticipated undie-droppage was to step daintily out of the offending pants and stow them in one's handbag.

Just as mortifyingly, a shortage of silk – coupled with the basic uselessness of cotton-lisle alternatives – meant that stockings simply weren't an option. But in the carelessly sexist climate of the time, neither were bare legs. The solution was a classic instance of the wartime make-do spirit: gravy browning. Or coffee. Or onion-skins. Or, if you could afford it, specially designed leg makeup ('gives bare legs the elegance of sheer silk!'). Anything to make one's legs stocking-coloured.

It was a tricky business. Even when you'd smeared on your gravy browning, you still had to ask a friend to draw on the seams.

In one way at least, the war brought life as well as death – in the form of antibiotics. Investment in these new wonder-drugs was boosted as the authorities struggled to respond to the staggering scale of casualties. So important was penicillin to the war effort that researchers working on the drug in the early 1940s smeared the miraculous mould on the linings of their suits in case the Germans invaded and they had to make a quick escape.

We all know that Alexander Fleming discovered penicillin ('mould-juice') growing in an unwashed petri dish. What's less well known is that his earlier discovery of the antiseptic lysozyme was also due to a revolting accident.

While Fleming, suffering from a heavy cold, was studying a dish of bacteria in his lab at St Mary's Medical School in London, a drop of his snot (Fleming's phlegm, if you prefer) dribbled out of his nose and into the dish. Naturally, he mixed the snot in with the bacteria to see what would happen.

The snot, wondrously, slowed the growth of the bacteria. The magic ingredient of the mucus was lysozome. Fleming would later call this his most important discovery. We have cause to be grateful for Fleming's slobbishness as well as his brilliance. If he'd done the washing up we'd never have had penicillin; if he'd had a clean hanky we'd never have heard of lysozome.

***

The Second World War, with which this chronicle of the strange but true in English history ends, was, like every war we've wandered through – and wondered at – in this book, a time of heroes (and villains. And people who weren't really either but just wanted to make it through the whole ghastly show and go home).

One man, perhaps, stands above the fray: Churchill.

Not Winston. We've heard enough from him already. Jack Churchill – Lieutenant Colonel 'Mad' Jack Churchill, to give him his full title – was, for the connoisseur of the odd but veritable, the most splendid hero of the war.

Churchill's finest early achievement as a soldier was crashing his motorbike into a water buffalo in Poona, India. That was only the beginning.

An outstanding player of the bagpipes and a world-class archer, Churchill was ideally suited to warfare, if the warfare in question happened to be taking place in the Middle Ages. He was called up to serve along the Maginot Line in 1939. Naturally, he took his bow and arrow with him, and spent the early years of the war picking off German soldiers with Agincourt-esque deadly aim.

After joining the commandos in 1941, Churchill extended his repertoire of historical lethalness by arming himself with a claymore, a two-handed longsword much in favour among sixteenth-century Scotsmen. On one night attack in the Adriatic, he led his men ashore while playing the bagpipes,[19] only to be shot and captured – recalling to mind Taillefer, the doomed instrument-strumming Norman minstrel-knight at Hastings, almost 1,000 years before.

'People are less likely to shoot you if you smile at them,' he once said. A motto for the ages.

The laws of this land have seldom made perfect sense.

In the 1600s you could be hanged for cutting down a tree (lucky for W.E. Gladstone he wasn't born 200 years earlier). In 1808, spending time 'in the company of gypsies' was a crime; if you were aged between 7 and 14, showing 'a strong evidence of malice' could be a capital offence. Right up until 9 November 2008, you could still be hanged in Britain for treason, or for being a pirate, or both.

Most startling of all was a law that would have made felons of six-eighths of the people featured in this book. Between 1824 and 2013, 'being an incorrigible rogue' was a criminal offence.

Endnotes

1 According to legend, the head was later found by Edmund's men, who were led to it by following the cries of a helpful wolf. Instead of chewing the ears off it and leaving the rest for the crows, the wolf called out 'here, here, here'. William Buckland could have told you that this is in no way typical wolf behaviour.

2 The Frenchness of de Montfort's proto-parliament persists in the modern-day Palace of Westminster: numerous forms of parliamentary communication – including endorsements on Bills ('soit baillé aux communes'), disagreements with Bills ('Ceste Bille est remise aux Seigneurs avecque des raisons') and Royal Assent ("La Reyne le veult') – are still written in Norman French.

3 'It is unfortunate,' the historian David Horspool has noted, 'that such desperate men [as Rookwood and Digby] are burdened with names that sound quite so effete to modern ears.'

4 We can joke about this now, but when the MP Sir John Coventry made a joke in the Commons about the king's fondness for ladies of the stage, soldiers were promptly despatched to ambush him on his way home and slit open his nose. 'Coventrying' was soon adopted as hoodlums' slang for this barbarous practice.

5 A similar inscription on London's monument to the Great Fire prompted the clear-sighted Alexander Pope to respond in verse: 'Where London's column, pointing at the skies/Like a tall bully, lifts the head and lies.'

6 Anagram fiends will notice at once that the letters of 'Georgian London' can be rearranged to spell 'O no, gin galore!' (yes, there are two letters left over, but everyone in Georgian London would have been too sloshed to notice).

7 He had died in 1616, bequeathing his wife his 'second-best bed' and penning an epitaph that warns everyone to leave his bones alone.

8 The Lord Chancellor has sat upon a wool-stuffed cushion
known as 'the Woolsack' since the reign of Edward III.
Back then, the wool was symbolic of England's world-leading
woollens industry. Today it would really be more accurate if the
Lord Chancellor sat on a cushion stuffed with North Sea gas or
financial services, but no, it's still wool.

9 10 Downing Street has been the official residence of the
First Lord of the Admiralty since 1735. Its last private resident
was a man named Mr Chicken. We don't know anything else
about him, but, really, his name is enough.

10 MPs in need of a tobacco hit at work have little other option:
smoking has been banned in and around the Commons
since 1693.

11 The navy wasn't always so proactive in embracing change.
In the First World War, the navy's battleships – travelling at
20 knots in formations 6 miles long – still communicated
using the same flag-signalling system used by Nelson's fleet
at Trafalgar.

12 We have to call him that because he was an aristocrat; if he
hadn't been, we could have called him a breathtakingly antisocial
yobbo. Even the Oxford Dictionary of National Biography lists
him as a 'landowner and reprobate'.

13 He seems to have been a surer shot than his father,
the 1st Marquess, who, out hunting pheasants one day,
shot someone's chicken by mistake.

14 Among the other things Gladstone did for fun were reforming
'fallen women' (hem, hem) and chopping down trees. Once he
got so carried away with his tree-chopping that he nearly
killed his son, who happened to be up the tree in question at
the time.

15 She also suggested that the reason why the Australians always
won at cricket was because they didn't drink as much as the
English. It's hard to know which side would find the idea
more offensive.

16 Mallory, who with Tenzing Norgay conquered the peak in 1953,
was also, in 1958, the first man to set foot at the South Pole since
Captain R.F. Scott in 1912.

17 Famous, and mispronounced. George Everest, the surveyor after whom the mountain was named in 1865, pronounced his name with two syllables, as 'Eve-rest'.

18 The pair had a complicated relationship. They admired one another greatly – though Lloyd George *did* say of Churchill that 'He would make a drum out of the skin of his mother in order to sound his own praises', which isn't a very friendly sentiment.

19 Another army bagpiper, Bill Millin, played the pipes while landing at Normandy on D-Day. The German soldiers didn't shoot him, because they thought he was mad.

If you enjoyed this book, you may also be interested in ...

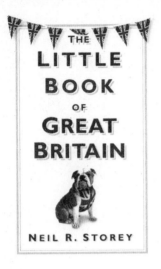

The Little Book of Great Britain

NEIL R. STOREY

This little gem of a book is a repository of intriguing, obscure and entertaining facts about Britain and all the things that make it great. This volume covers legends, traditions and customs as well as music, food, entertainment and sport, to name just a few. Discover some unusual pub names, the name of Her Majesty Queen Elizabeth II's first corgi, and the name of Britain's first person to be convicted of speeding – in 1896. Neil R. Storey is an author and historian based in Norfolk. He has written numerous titles on such varied topics as crime, local and national history and trivia.

978 0 7524 7114 3

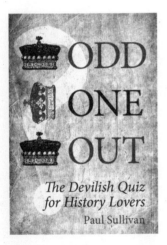

Odd One Out

PAUL SULLIVAN

Can you guess:

Which historical leader banned moustaches? Which British king was thought to be a werewolf? Which man was 'the most efficient executioner in British history'? Which Scottish monster is said to be an omen of death?

This amazing little quiz book contains sixty different 'odd one outs' from history for you to test your wits against. Try it today and find out just how much you really know about Great Britain's past ...

978 0 7509 5572 0

Visit our website and discover thousands of other History Press books.

www.thehistorypress.co.uk

The History Press